THE POWER OF YOUR FAITH

Dr. Howard E. Anderson, Sr.

The Power of Your Faith
by Howard E. Anderson, Sr.
ISBN 978-0-9903477-5-0

Published by Austin Brothers Publishing
Fort Worth, Texas
www.austinbrotherspublishing.com

Printed in the United States of America

All Scripture quotes are taken from the New Kings James Version (NKJV) unless otherwise indicated.

This and other books published by
Austin Brothers Publishing can be purchased at
www.austinbrotherspublishing.com

I affectionately dedicate this book to my lovely wife Shirley, God's great gift to our family and my encourager, counselor, supporter and best friend for 49 years.

To my son Howard E. Anderson, Jr., M.D., his wife Erica, and my precious Grandchildren, Francesca Von, Howard III, and William Albert

To the loving memories of the Anderson, Williams, Anthony and Culton family members

To the staff and congregation of the "Exciting" Singing Hills Baptist Church for your love, prayers, and support.

To all who will read this book.

I acknowledge and thank my editor Terry Austin for helping to make this book a reality.

I humbly acknowledge Jesus Christ as my Savior and Lord, and thank the Holy Spirit for His guiding presence and guarding power in my life.

Contents

Introduction	1
The Call of Faith	5
The Enabling Power of Faith	15
The Accessing Power of Faith	27
The Purposeful Power of Faith	39
The Participating Power of Faith	51
The Perspective of Faith	61
The Proving Power of Faith	73
The Secret to Walking by Faith	83
Testing Your Faith	93
Keeping Your Faith Powerful	107
A Beyond Faith	117
About the Author	121

Introduction

One of the great blessings of being a pastor is being present with people during some of the most powerful events of their life. Often it is a joyous time, like a wedding, new birth, anniversary celebration, award ceremony, or a spiritual rebirth. These occasions speak for themselves, and I discovered, as a pastor, that I am just along for the ride. They don't need a spiritual interpreter, counselor, or consoler. In fact, the pastor might be invited as a good friend of the family, or as the one responsible for bringing God into the room, just like Aunt Martha is bringing the potato salad.

If that was all there was to being a pastor the line to sign up for seminary would be mighty long. The reality is that for every event of celebration and rejoicing, a pastor must also be present dozens of times when it feels like there will never be rejoicing again. These are times of loss and struggle, loneliness and pain, disillusionment and depression, and perhaps even despair and death.

It is during those times that a pastor is more than an emissary of God bringing greetings and well wishes into the room. The pastor is there to answer unanswerable questions, point the way to elusive hope, and turn the world right-side-up once again. Essentially, the pastor is expected to do the impossible. I have been there many times. I have been there walking alongside others, and I have been there walking along my own path of life.

Yet, there are other times when a pastor's advice is sought for making life decisions and giving directions. These are exciting moments when future success or failure hangs in the balance. These are the moments of decision, when we step out and walk with God, or step aside and let spiritual life pass us by.

Along the way I have discovered an amazing resource—faith.

- By faith you can see what you have never seen
- By faith you can do what you have never done
- By faith you can go where you have never gone
- By faith you can learn what you have never known
- By faith you can hear what you have never heard
- By faith you can speak what you have never spoken

Jesus taught us about the power of faith. He answered the Disciples' question about failure by saying, *Because of your unbelief; for assuredly, I say to you, if you have faith as a mustard seed, you will say to this mountain, 'Move from here to there,' and it will move; and nothing will be impossible for you.* (Matthew 17:20).

The context of His statement is the disappointment of the Disciples. They had encountered a young boy who was demon possessed. When they failed to exorcise the demon, they came to Jesus to figure out why. He had already given them authority to do so, but why did they fail? Jesus told them it was because their faith was too little.

Before they can even ask what you think might be the next question, Jesus provided the answer. You would expect them to ask, "How much faith do we need?"

So Jesus says all they need is faith as small as a mustard seed. The mustard seed is one of the smallest plant seeds. It can grow into a significant bush, but the seed that contains the mustard plant is very tiny. In other words, Jesus is saying you don't need much because faith is very powerful.

Mustard seed faith not only suggests size in the sense that God honors even a little faith, but it also has the connotation of life and growth. It is faith that is alive. In order for a mustard seed to sprout into a full-grown bush, it must be cultivated. Our faith also must be cultivated before it can reach full potential.

I can assure you that I have been in the same situation experienced by the Disciples, trying to understand failure. I have spent years of ministry striving to understand what makes life possible. What I have learned is that Jesus is correct. The key to doing the things God has called us to do is faith. It is not an easy lesson to learn, but there is tremendous power in our faith.

This book was born out of my 35 years of preaching. But, my preaching was born in hospital rooms, nursing homes, living rooms, courtrooms, funeral homes, and any place else where I have been with people and their families in the midst of trials. Through it all I have learned the power of faith.

Faith not only carries us through the difficulties of life, it also equips us for the challenges of life. We will confront many opportunities that require us to step forward with nothing more than our belief that God is going before us.

I invite you to join me for the journey. Through the next few pages, we are going to walk with many of the characters of the Bible, the ones often classified as great heroes of faith. We will learn what made them tick, and hopefully discover the secrets that can allow us to enjoy the power of faith. I can assure you it will be an exciting adventure.

Chapter One

The Call of Faith

Now the LORD said to Abram, "Go forth from your country, And from your relatives And from your father's house, To the land which I will show you; And I will make you a great nation, And I will bless you, And make your name great; And so you shall be a blessing; And I will bless those who bless you, And the one who curses you I will curse. And in you all the families of the earth will be blessed." So Abram went forth as the LORD had spoken to him; and Lot went with him. Now Abram was seventy-five years old when he departed from Haran. (Genesis 12:1-4)

More than 30 years ago, when the The Singing Hills Baptist Church was organized, we met in the Moorland Branch YMCA in Dallas, TX. We named the church Singing Hills Baptist Church because that is the neighborhood were God called us to minister. We didn't have an inch of property in the Singing Hills Community. The *Enemy* suggested that if the church had another name, we could buy property somewhere else. However, I believed in my heart that God wanted the church to be planted in the Singing Hills Community. Therefore, we kept praying and searching for property with the power of our faith in God.

One day, driving down what was Houston School Road, I saw a real estate sign stating property for sale. I called the agent about the property and he said, "God must have this property for your church because no one has inquired about the property but you."

His statement was merely a confirmation of what we believed. It was a confirmation of our faith. We give glory to God for allowing us to purchase the property in the Singing Hills Community.

The story of The *Exciting* Singing Hills Baptist Church from the beginning to the present has been about the power of our faith in God.

Responding to God's call to move to a new situation is usually a difficult task. My call to start a new church is similar to Abram's call to a new place. Both required saying goodbye to comfortable situations. Both required faith. It's not easy to say goodbye to friends, a home, a job, and a neighborhood where we feel at home. Even when we are not in the best of circumstances, deciding to respond to such a call can be a challenge.

Yet, that is exactly what happens when God calls us to follow Him in faith. The story of Abram's call to leave his home is the story of all of us. We must leave the past behind in order to follow Him. This can only be done with faith.

In order to get to where God wants us to be, we have to leave where we are.

God called Abram to leave his home and family. He had to leave everything behind, all the things that would hold him back. He had to walk away from everything that provided security. Home is the most comfortable place in our lives. It is the place where we feel safe, where we can relax. Whenever we leave home, we are leaving something important behind. Whether you are walking out the door for just a few hours or an extended absence, it doesn't matter; leaving home produces a feeling of emptiness and aloneness.

Do you recall the first time you left home? Perhaps it was when you finished high school and set off to attend college, or perhaps when you got a job that would pay enough to find your own place. For many, this adventure begins when they get married or change jobs. Regardless of when it happens, it is a little frightening to realize that you are on your own.

It is much easier to leave home when we are young. We are expected to leave home, start our own life, and create another home. However, Abram was not a young man just starting out. He was 75 years old. Even a young person can appreciate making such a significant change after you have invested your life in one place for seven and a half decades. Don't forget, this was a time when moving was not done with a U-Haul. For Abram, moving meant organizing a caravan of camels and other beasts of burden, and an enormous amount of walking. Not an easy task for an already old man.

On top of that, he had to go without knowing where, to a land *which I will show you.* He had to learn to live in continual dependence upon God. The reason he had to leave home was because God had someplace else for him to be. In order to be where God wanted him, Abram had to leave home.

The reason he had to leave home was because God had someplace else for him to be.

If you have travelled in East Texas, or some other heavily wooded area, you have probably found yourself feeling that where you are going is a place where you can't get to from where you are. It seems there are too many obstacles between you and where you want to be, or the road just doesn't go where you want to go. When that occurs, the only workable course of action is to move and start somewhere else.

That is what Abram had to do. God wanted him to be at a certain place, but until Abram was willing to leave his father's home, he could not get to where God wanted him to be. Just as Abram had to leave everything, so do we—our family, land, possessions, friends, accomplishments, failures, struggles, hopes, and dreams.

When I speak of home, it is not necessarily the house where we live. I am referring to the things we turn to for security, the things that hold us back and keep us from serving God. For example, it might mean we have to leave behind an experience that we have repeatedly used as an excuse for failure. We have said things like "I can't do that because I was abused" (or mistreated, or handicapped). Or, it might be a place where we retreat when the going gets tough, like food, harmful relationships, or unhealthy activities. For some it might be an attitude such as "I am a failure," or "I'm weak" or powerless, or worthless.

In fact, it is probably easier to leave tangible things like houses and jobs, than intangible things like attitudes and feelings.

The point of all this, and the truth that Abram realized, is that you cannot simply squeeze God into your current life. In order to experience all the things God has for us, we must be willing to leave where we are. This is the same message Jesus delivered to His Disciples. *When He had called the people to Himself, with His disciples also, He said to them, "Whoever desires to come after Me, let him deny himself, and take up his cross, and follow Me.* (Mark 8:34)

When we are willing to go where God wants us to be, there are great blessings for us and others.

One of the reasons we are unable to let go of the present is because we are not sure it will be worth the cost. Leaving home, giving up our source of security and comfort is a risky thing. We must be convinced that it is worth the risk.

Abram was given a great promise by God if he would simply leave home. It was a promise that impacted Abram and all mankind. However, in order to grab hold of God's promise, he had to walk away from everything else. It might sound trite, but you cannot get to somewhere else until you leave where you are.

The promise to Abram was fantastic. He was told he would become a great nation, be blessed, have a great name, and be a blessing to others. The language is written in such a way as to emphasize the ascending nature of each promise. It begins with an increase from one man to a numerous people, a great nation.

Next, the blessing refers to material and spiritual prosperity, both of which Abram eventually enjoyed. The exaltation of his name refers to being elevated to a position of honor and glory. Finally, he was to be a possessor and dispenser of blessings. In other words, others would be blessed or cursed, depending on their relationship with Abram. The promise made to Abram extended to every person who will ever live.

What God was offering to do for Abram could not happen if he chose to stay at home. If he would have chosen the comfort and security of home, he might have lived another few years tending his sheep and then died in obscurity. His life would have made very little impact on the world.

What if Noah would have ignored God's call to be a shipbuilder, choosing instead to enjoy the respect of his community? What if David would have stayed in the pasture rather than going to the battle field to confront Goliath? What if Columbus would have stayed on the safety of the European coast, rather than heading across the Atlantic? What if Martin Luther would have chosen the quiet safety of a German monastery rather than traveling to Rome to confront the Vatican? What if Martin Luther King Jr. would have chosen to be a quiet parish pastor rather than the front lines of the racial debate?

I don't know for sure, but I think if God's people would have chosen not to leave home and venture into the unknown, God would have found another way. His purpose cannot be thwarted. However, the loser is not God, but the one who refuses to follow God.

God comes to all of us, calling us to leave the past and the present behind in order to be where He wants us to be. Some follow, some don't. *Then Peter began to say to Him, "See, we have left all and followed You." So Jesus answered and said, "Assuredly, I say to you, there is no one who has left house or brothers or sisters or father or mother or wife or children or lands, for My sake and the gospel's, who shall not receive a hundredfold now in this time—houses and brothers and sisters and mothers and children and lands, with persecutions—and in the age to come, eternal life. But many who are first will be last, and the last first."* (Mark 10:28-31)

We cannot lose when we are willing to be where God wants us to be!

The only way to get to where God want us to be is to take the first step.

So Abram went forth as the LORD had spoken to him... From that moment on, Abram's life was totally changed, even his name was eventually changed. He became the father of a nation, the head of a world religion, and the leader of the people of God. All of this occurred because he took the first step.

We are all familiar with Neal Armstrong, the first man to walk on the moon. On July 21, 1969, he made that memorable statement—"That's one small step for [a] man, one giant leap for mankind."

Martin Luther King Jr., said, "Faith is taking the first step even when you don't see the whole staircase."

> Martin Luther King Jr., said, "Faith is taking the first step even when you don't see the whole staircase."

If we never take the first step, we will never leave where we are in order to get to where God wants us to be. If you want to be the person God wants you to be, you must take the first step. He does not drag us, kicking and screaming. He calls us to follow Him. The first step is our choice.

We have all been called to live a life of faith. It is unlikely that God is calling you to leave your family and home to relocate in another part of the world (unlikely, but not impossible). However, He is calling you to put aside everything that keeps you from following Him. That is the purpose of this book—to help you understand what an amazing resource God has given to you that we call faith, and then how to appropriate its power.

Essentially I am inviting you to join me on the journey of faith. It is a trip that will take us to amazing parts unknown and beyond our comprehension. Picture yourself like Abram—a shepherd from an obscure village with little hope of becoming anything more than a wandering shepherd. Yet, look what faith did for him. It is the same faith that can and will do wonderful things for you and me.

Chapter Two

The Enabling Power of Faith

By faith Moses, when he was born, was hidden for three months by his parents, because they saw he was a beautiful child; and they were not afraid of the king's edict. By faith Moses, when he had grown up, refused to be called the son of Pharaoh's daughter, choosing rather to endure ill-treatment with the people of God than to enjoy the passing pleasures of sin, considering the reproach of Christ greater riches than the treasures of Egypt; for he was looking to the reward.

By faith he left Egypt, not fearing the wrath of the king; for he endured, as seeing Him who is unseen. By faith he kept the Passover and the sprinkling of the blood, so that he who destroyed the firstborn would not touch them. By faith they passed through the Red Sea as though they were passing through dry land; and the Egyptians, when they attempted it, were drowned. (Hebrews 11:23-29)

Hebrews chapter eleven is considered one of the greatest statements about faith ever recorded. It contains theological statements, historical accounts, and practical guidance that has become a crucial volume in the library of the church.

The segment that is the focus of this chapter is the story of Moses, and his powerful example of faith. It is one of the greatest adventures of all time, the subject of several motion pictures over the years. It is also one of the greatest "Rags to Riches" stories ever.

Moses was born to a young Hebrew woman at the worst possible time. The Hebrews were perceived as a threat to their Egyptian captors. In order to hold down the increasing number of slaves, the Egyptians issued an order that all male babies were to be killed. The Bible presents a fascinating account of how God intervened, and preserved the life of the infant Moses (see Exodus 1:15-22).

The baby was hidden for three months. However, the time came when it was no longer possible, so he was placed in a carefully constructed basket, and positioned in the river in hopes that something miraculous would happen. It did.

The daughter of Pharaoh, the Egyptian king, discovered the child. In defiance of her father's edict, she instructed her servants to care for the baby, even enlisting his actual mother to be his nurse. An amazing story! A child born to a family of slaves under the order of death is raised in the king's own household.

We would like to know more details about the life of young Moses in the house of Pharaoh, but we are told very little. The one thing we are told is that he was aware of his heritage—he knew he was a Hebrew.

One day he noticed an overzealous Egyptian taskmaster taking one of his kinsmen to task. Moses intervened, and killed the Egyptian. He took matters into his own hands. Perhaps there was something in his heart that told him he was to be the one to free his people. If that was the case, he was not up to the task.

When word got out about what he had done, Moses was afraid, and ran away into the desert. He spent the next couple of decades tending sheep and raising a family far away from the Egyptians.

This story has all the elements of a great tale. Born in slavery and poverty—raised in power and wealth—haunted by his true identity—striving to find peace as a nobody in the wilderness—minding his own business. This man, hiding in the wilderness due to fear, is about to become the greatest leader in the history of God's people.

How did it happen?

That is the subject of this chapter. Moses succeeded, not because of his birth, his upbringing, or his great skill. It was because of his faith. As we focus on the faith of Moses, we will think about the power of our faith in God

Now faith is the substance of things hoped for, the evidence of things not seen. For by it the elders obtained a good testimony.

But without faith it is impossible to please Him, for he who comes to God must believe that He is, and that He is a rewarder of those who diligently seek Him.

By faith Moses, when he became of age, refused to be called the son of Pharaoh's daughter, choosing rather to suffer affliction with the people of God than to enjoy the passing pleasures of sin... (Hebrews 11:1-2,6,24-25)

Moses, like all the others listed in the eleventh chapter of the Book of Hebrews, thought it was better to suffer for Christ than to have all the rewards of Egypt. There is amazing power in faith when you have placed it in God.

The Christian life is based upon faith. It begins with the necessity of having faith in God. We know that we cannot see Him physically, but by faith we are able to put our trust in Him.

Faith, as it will be defined in this book, is the substance we hope for or the ground or support that we stand upon. Faith to the Christian is what a foundation is to a house. Without a foundation it will not stand.

The writer of Hebrews also uses the word "evidence" to describe faith (see 11:1). Evidence equals conviction, the sureness that God is real. We can put our trust in Him. We can put our weight upon Him. He has never failed. There is no failure in God.

When we look at the life of Moses we can't help but see the faith of his mother and father as they did not listen to the king (see 11:23). It was their faith that allowed them to see the beauty of their son, and to be fearless of Pharaoh. So Moses grew up as a child of faith. Even though his parents did not have daily influence over him for a long time, he never forgot, somehow, who God was. The courage to stand in defiance of man with faith in God is a quality that characterized both Moses and his parents.

When he matured, he refused the call to be a son of Pharaoh's daughter. The power of faith is the power to refuse something. Listen carefully because this is extremely important. Faith is the power to refuse something—to refuse to do something, to say something, to believe something, or to tie into the activities of the world. This is not a small thing.

When we don't have faith in God, we are constantly in danger of falling for something. The world says the path to success is to have certain things, or to act certain ways. The world says the way to be somebody is to have certain qualities and traits. The world says only intelligent people believe certain things. However, faith give us the ability to refuse the things of the world, and instead, choose the things of God.

God's way and the world's way are often at odds, pulling in opposite directions. Without faith we have no ability to resist the pull of the world. But with faith comes the power to refuse.

Moses had an inheritance; he was in line to receive all that Pharaoh had, the inheritance of a king. He was willing and able to put that aside, not because of his great willpower or inner character, but because of his faith. He was willing to put that aside, not worried about prestige, because he believed God. When you have faith in God you can refuse to tie into material things for prestige.

Moses also refused the position. The world is always self-promoting. We are constantly encouraged to put ourselves out there, promote ourselves, show others who we are and what we can do. Because of his faith, Moses was able to refuse to do that. He did not want to be the son of the king. He refused the kingdom of the world, and chose instead the kingdom of God.

If you have faith, there is no need to self promote because we are not about the world. That is why we study the life and faith of Moses. He speaks to us today, so that we can refuse the things of this world. We can live by the same faith that carried him. Our trust, like his, is not in the things of the world, but in God.

Those who humble themselves, God will exalt. Moses refused the treasures of Egypt. He said, "I don't want any part of it."

How is that possible, you ask. Because he had faith in God. His trust was in something much greater than what the world has to offer, even to the son of a king.

You are also able to choose. When you refuse something, it means you are choosing something else. Moses chose to suffer affliction rather than enjoy the passing pleasures of sin.

Everything we see around us is temporary, even if it is the wealth of a king. Everything around us is passing away. We live in a world that is not standing still, it is fading away. There were a lot of things in Pharaoh's house, but Moses refused them because he looked at another reward that was even greater (v.26). He had faith that his reward was from God, and nothing on earth could possibly compare.

The same faith that characterized Moses' life can also characterize your life. Your faith in God gives you the ability and opportunity to please God (11:6). Here is how it works: faith is our response to God's Word through obedience. The power of our faith (our response to God) enables us to do as Moses did. The power of Moses' faith in God allowed him to refuse, to choose, to esteem, and to forsake things in life based upon his relationship with God (11:24-27). This kind of faith is a gift from God. *For I say, through the grace given to me, to everyone who is among you, not to think of himself more highly than he ought to think, but to think soberly, as God has dealt to each one a measure of faith.* (Romans 12:3)

Your faith in God gives you the ability and opportunity to please God.

This kind of faith will enable you to see beyond the circumstances of your life. Let's focus on Moses again, particularly the circumstances of his life. As a child and a young man, these circumstances indicated he had the potential of being one of the wealthiest and most powerful men in the world. Yet, the truth is that none of these things the world had to offer was the path to greatness for Moses. With the eyes of faith, he was able to look beyond them to see something much more valuable.

When Moses looked beyond his earthly circumstances he saw that the hand of God was upon him

> *So they sent and gathered together all the lords of the Philistines, and said, "Send away the ark of the God of Israel,*

> *and let it go back to its own place, so that it does not kill us and our people." For there was a deadly destruction throughout all the city; the hand of God was very heavy there.* (1 Samuel 5:11)

> *...by the good hand of our God upon us, they brought us a man of understanding...* (Ezra 8:18)

This is an amazing thing when you consider all the practical ramifications. When our eyes are focused on our circumstances, life is a struggle. We see poor health, insurmountable financial problems, painful relationships, and impossible challenges. All we can see are the things that drag us down and rob us of the power and possibility to do anything significant.

However, faith opens us to those things that are beyond our circumstances. Instead of our poor health, we see the Great Physician. Instead of financial problems, we see the One who has promised to meet our every need. Instead of painful relationships, we see a Savior who loves us unconditionally. Instead of impossible challenges, we see the possibility of moving mountains.

> *So Jesus answered and said to them, "Have faith in God. For assuredly, I say to you, whoever says to this mountain, 'Be removed and be cast into the sea,' and does not doubt in his heart, but believes that those things he says will be done, he will have whatever he says. "Have faith in God,"* (Mark 11:22-23)

Jesus is speaking about the same quality of faith that was possessed by Moses. It is the same kind of faith that is available to you and me. The circumstances in your life might look like a mountain standing in your way, but faith says, "Look past the mountain!"

Another characteristic of faith is that it will enable you to see beyond the consequences of your life. Everything we do has a consequence—good or bad. But, we must learn to look beyond consequences. The first thing we will see is the help of God. When things are coming at us so fast, it requires faith. It will enable you to look beyond the consequences and see the help of God. That's good news.

God is our refuge and strength,
A very present help in trouble.
Therefore we will not fear,
Even though the earth be removed,
And though the mountains be carried into the midst of the sea;
Though its waters roar and be troubled,
Though the mountains shake with its swelling. Selah
There is a river whose streams shall make glad the city of God,
The holy place of the tabernacle of the Most High.
God is in the midst of her, she shall not be moved;
God shall help her, just at the break of dawn.
The nations raged, the kingdoms were moved;
He uttered His voice, the earth melted.
The Lord of hosts is with us;
The God of Jacob is our refuge. (Psalm 46:1-7)

The Psalmist reminds us that God is a very present help. There is no need to wait until the end of the month, next week, or next year. He is a very present help. Faith gives us eyes to see this powerful truth.

We are often paralyzed from acting because of our fear of the consequences. Look at Moses. God called him to stand before Pharaoh and demand the freedom of his people. The obvious consequences of such a treasonous act would appear to be swift and devastating. Yet, because of his faith, Moses was able to see beyond the consequences. He did not see the mountain; he saw the hand of God.

> Each of those great Bible characters knew they were only pilgrims passing through a barren land. Life on this side will surely end.

How often are you discouraged and defeated, even before you attempt something, because all you can see are the consequences of your action? God has called you to speak out on His behalf, yet you remain quiet because of what others might say. God has called you to give generously, yet you keep your hands tightly closed because of the fear of needing it yourself.

A third possibility of faith is that it will enable you to see beyond the conclusion of your life. All of the great Heroes of Faith listed in Hebrews 11 died before they realized the promise of God (see 11:13). Even though they died before seeing the promise, they believed in the promise. They knew the words of the song even before it was written—

This world is not my home
I'm just a-passing through
My treasures are laid up
Somewhere beyond the blue.

Each of those great Bible characters knew they were only pilgrims passing through a barren land. Life on this side will surely end.

Rejoice that you have faith in the Lord. The end is coming, but you have another home. The Apostle Paul reminded us that we have a building of God not made with hands). One day, life ends on this side, but we have a home on the other side. Jesus said you believe in God believe also in me, for in my father's house are many mansions.

> *For we know that if our earthly house, this tent, is destroyed, we have a building from God, a house not made with hands, eternal in the heavens.* (2 Corinthians 5:1)

> *In My Father's house are many mansions; if it were not so, I would have told you. I go to prepare a place for you.* (John 14:2)

When you put your faith in God, you have a beyond faith: a faith that is beyond who you are, beyond what you have, beyond what you know, beyond what you feel, beyond what you can do, beyond what you think, and beyond what you see. Faith looks beyond the present to a future with God.

When we see the possibility of faith in God, it is clear why the great list of faithful saints recorded in the Book of Hebrews accomplished so many things. As we work our way through our study of faith, we will not only discover what faith has done for those who have gone before us, but also what it can do for us today.

What it means to be a follower of Jesus is that we have learned to *walk by faith, not by sight* (2 Corinthians

5:7). When Paul wrote those words to the Corinthians, centuries before our time, and centuries after Moses' time, he was building on the foundation that had been laid by Moses and many others. Moses did not live his life according to the things he could see. Rather, he built his life on the things he could only see through the lens of faith.

We can now understand what the writer means as he defines faith. It *is the substance of things hoped for, the evidence of things not seen.* (Hebrews 11:1) It is choosing to live according to the word of God, not the worries of the world. It is following in the footsteps of Moses, and men and women like him, those who have gone before us, and demonstrated what it means to live by faith.

It is a journey; but it is an exciting journey.

Chapter Three

The Accessing Power of Faith

By faith the people passed through the Red Sea as on dry land; but when the Egyptians tried to do so, they were drowned. (Hebrews 11:29)

Now the Lord spoke to Moses, saying: "Speak to the children of Israel, that they turn and camp before Pi Hahiroth, between Migdol and the sea, opposite Baal Zephon; you shall camp before it by the sea. For Pharaoh will say of the children of Israel, 'They are bewildered by the land; the wilderness has closed them in.' Then I will harden Pharaoh's heart, so that he will pursue them; and I will gain honor over Pharaoh and over all his army, that the Egyptians may know that I am the Lord." And they did so.

Now it was told the king of Egypt that the people had fled, and the heart of Pharaoh and his servants was turned against the people; and they said, "Why have we done this, that we have let Israel go from serving us?" So he made ready his chariot and took his people with him. Also, he took six hundred choice chariots, and all the chariots of Egypt with captains over every one of them. And the Lord hardened the heart of Pharaoh king of Egypt, and he pursued the children of Israel; and the children of Israel went out with boldness. So the Egyptians pursued them, all the horses and chariots of Pharaoh, his horsemen and his army, and overtook them camping by the sea beside Pi Hahiroth, before Baal Zephon.

And when Pharaoh drew near, the children of Israel lifted their eyes, and behold, the Egyptians marched after them. So they were very afraid, and the children of Israel cried out to the Lord. Then they said to Moses, "Because there were no graves in Egypt, have you taken us away to die in the wilderness? Why have you so dealt with us, to bring us up out of Egypt? Is this not the word that we told you in Egypt, saying, 'Let us alone that we may serve the Egyptians'? For it would have been better for us to serve the Egyptians than that we should die in the wilderness."

And Moses said to the people, "Do not be afraid. Stand still, and see the salvation of the Lord, which He will accomplish for you today. For the Egyptians whom you see today, you shall see again no more forever. The Lord will fight for you, and you shall hold your peace."

And the Lord said to Moses, "Why do you cry to Me? Tell the children of Israel to go forward. But lift up your rod, and stretch out your hand over the sea and divide it. And the children of Israel shall go on dry ground through the midst of the sea. And I indeed will harden the hearts of the Egyptians, and they shall follow them. So I will gain honor over Pharaoh and over all his army, his chariots, and his horsemen. Then the Egyptians shall know that I am the Lord, when I have gained honor for Myself over Pharaoh, his chariots, and his horsemen."

And the Angel of God, who went before the camp of Israel, moved and went behind them; and the pillar of cloud went from before them and stood behind them. (Exodus 14:1-19)

This story of Moses leading the Israelites out of Egypt is the ultimate example of being stuck between a rock and a hard place. In front of the massive parade of people fleeing Egyptian slavery is the uncrossable Red Sea. To the rear, and coming up fast, is the army of Pharaoh, probably the most powerful military force of the day.

I know you have been in that same place in your life. You know what it is like to stand face to face with an immovable obstacle that keeps you from moving forward, and simultaneously surrounded by overwhelming problems. What's a person to do? Moses, the man of faith, will show us.

What we learn from Moses is that faith gives us access. The word "access" means the ability, right, or commission to approach, to enter, or to speak. It is through faith that we have access to approach the throne of God. This means we can speak to God. Faith is the door that gives us entrance into His kingdom.

One of the primary reasons Moses encountered problems in leading the children of Israel out of Egypt is that Pharaoh enjoyed the servitude of the Hebrews. Letting go of as many as a million slaves was not an easy thing. But

Moses had something the Egyptians did not have, he had access to God.

God utilized a cloud during the day and a fire during the night to lead them. It was the angel of God moving before them and working behind them. The pillar moved and stood between them and the hostile army. They were guarded from behind. But God also led them from in front.

At the beginning of this story, it seems that God led them in a pattern that made it appear they were lost, aimlessly wandering in the desert. The purpose was to inspire Pharaoh to continue his pursuit. It was as if God wanted the Egyptians to pursue the Israelites. He was setting them up so he could show them and the Israelites that he was the Lord. He was creating a situation so that only He could receive the glory.

We often find ourselves in situations that seem impossible to resolve, facing a need that is beyond our reach. It might be that God wants us to be in exactly that situation so we can recognize Him and His provision. When life is too smooth, and everything working exactly like we desire, it is tempting to forget God.

This is the warning God gave to His people upon entering the Promised Land.

> *So it shall be, when the Lord your God brings you into the land of which He swore to your fathers, to Abraham, Isaac, and Jacob, to give you large and beautiful cities which you did not build, houses full of all good things, which you did not fill, hewn-out wells which you did not dig, vineyards and olive trees which you did not plant—when you have eaten and are full—then beware, lest you forget the Lord who brought you out of*

the land of Egypt, from the house of bondage. (Deuteronomy 6:10-12)

If you are anything like me, you will find it is easier to seek God's presence and provisions when things are difficult than when things are smooth.

So, it is not surprising when Moses and the Israelites found themselves in an impossible situation, they *cried out to the Lord*. For the people it was a cry of defeat and desperation. Do you hear the despair in their words—"Was it because there were no graves in Egypt that you brought us to the desert to die? What have you done to us by bringing us out of Egypt? Didn't we say to you in Egypt, *Leave us alone; let us serve the Egyptians'? It would have been better for us to serve the Egyptians than to die in the desert* (verses 11-13).

They had completely given up, and resorted to arguing about whether it was better to die in Egypt as slaves, or in the wilderness as refugees. The only thing certain, in their minds, was death.

> If God is going to work on our behalf then we must learn to be still and trust him.

But, for Moses it was not a cry of defeat and desperation—it was a cry of faith. By faith, Moses stretched out his arms, reaching heavenward with his rod, and God opened the sea. Before he did, however, he offered a powerful directive to the Israelites. He told them that God would take care of their problem and what they needed to do was *be still* (verse 14).

These are great words of faith. If God is going to work on our behalf then we must learn to be still and trust him. Perhaps the reason God is not able to work with you is because you are too busy trying to do it all yourself. You might be running around shaking every doorknob and looking behind every bush for a solution to your problem. Try this—be still and trust in God.

God was working. The angel of God moved and went behind them. The pillar moved and stood behind them. God was involved in the process. By faith Moses stretched out his rod, and God opened the sea. As God opened the sea, behind them was the angel of God, and the pillar of clouds blocking the view of the Egyptians who could not see what God was doing. As they moved through the sea on dry ground the Egyptians followed, expecting their feet to stand on the same dry earth.

God troubled them and pulled the wheels off the chariots and allowed the water to drown them. The entire Egyptian army, including horses and chariots, all drowned in the sea. I remember a song from my days of singing with the youth choir...

> Oh Mary don't you weep
> Tell Martha not to moan
> Pharaoh's army got drowned in the Red Sea

This is the story of Moses' faith, the story of your faith, and my faith. The same faith we can all share when we place it in Jesus Christ. It is a faith that provides access to God's power.

Your faith provides access to God's presence

God's presence is a significant thing. I understand that because He is God, He is present everywhere at all times. Here I am speaking of God's presence in the sense that we know He is here. To have access to God's presence means we have the ability to communicate with Him. We can speak to Him, and we can hear when He speaks to us through His Spirit.

One of the biggest assets Moses had was his faith that allowed him access to God's presence. His faith gave him the ability to cry out to God. It also gave him the ability to receive God's leadership. It is a marvelous thing to walk in the presence of God.

Moses first accessed God's presence at the burning bush. He was instructed by God to tell Pharaoh to free the children and allow them to move on. When we pray, we are accessing God's presence. It is a privilege we have because of our relationship with Him. We can go to Him at anytime through prayer. Jesus instructed His Disciples with the words, *when you pray*. This prayer gives us access and we are instructed to say, *our Father...*

When we call upon Him, we are able to access His presence. God's presence is no small thing. Consider David when he got in trouble with Bathsheba, and Nathan pointed out his sin. *Do not cast me from your presence or take your Holy Spirit from me* (Psalm 51:11). Like David, we must never take access to His presence lightly.

Your faith provides access to God's path

The Red Sea was the path God chose for the Children of Israel to leave Egypt. It would certainly not have been the first choice of Moses. Think about it. He just completed the long arduous task of confronting Pharaoh and securing the release of the Israelites. There is no way he would have chosen to lead the newly freed people straight into the sea. This would never have been Moses' path.

> His path is far beyond our ability to find and follow on our own. Yet, through faith, we not only discover God's path, we also are able to walk down His path.

Crossing the Red Sea was certainly God's path, and Moses accepted it because of his faith. God brought them to and through the Red Sea, and it reminds us that whatever He brings us to He is able to bring us through. If God brings you to a place, He is able to bring you through that place.

God led them through the sea into the wilderness so He could get them to the Promised Land. They did not go into the wilderness on their own understanding, but because they were following God's path. Who would not want to have access to God's path? He is the One who gives direction.

It is through faith that we access the path God has set before us.

Trust in the Lord with all your heart
and lean not on your own understanding;

in all your ways submit to him,
and he will make your paths straight. (Proverbs 3:5-6 NIV)

It is clear why we need faith to access God's path. "For my thoughts are not your thoughts, neither are your ways my ways," declares the LORD (Isaiah 55:8). His path is far beyond our ability to find and follow on our own. Yet, through faith, we not only discover God's path, we also are able to walk down His path.

Your faith provides access to God's promises

Imagine yourself standing on the damp shore of the Red Sea with a rising cloud of dust kicked up by the Egyptian chariots coming up behind you, and you hear Moses, your leader say, *Do not be afraid. Stand still, and see the salvation of the Lord, which He will accomplish for you today. For the Egyptians whom you see today, you shall see again no more forever.* (Exodus 14:13) All the obstacles and barriers that surround you are about to be removed.

This is the access you have through faith. It is access to the promises of God. God's Word is filled with promises, but they are not available to all people. They are only accessed by faith.

Blessed be the Lord, who has given rest to His people Israel, according to all that He promised. There has not failed one word of all His good promise, which He promised through His servant Moses. (1 Kings 8:56)

Not one of His promises that He gave to Moses failed because Moses had access to them through his faith.

Your faith provides access to God's power

The Red Sea rolled back on each side. By faith, they passed through the middle on dry land. The Egyptians, attempting to do the same thing, were drowned. What Israel did by faith, the Egyptians thought they could do by presumption. Because they had more people, power, and chariots, they thought they could also pass through the sea. All they saw was dry ground, and weak runaway slaves.

Once they crossed the sea, God told Moses to stretch out his rod, and when he did, the water covered the Egyptians (see Zechariah 4:6). It was evident to everyone there that this was a miracle of God. There was no doubt that God had acted on their behalf with an amazing demonstration of His power.

This is the power that is accessed by faith. It is not power that we can possess to allow us to do things on our own. Instead, it is the power of God. When we live our lives with faith in Him then His power is available to accomplish His will. It is the faith described by Jesus when he said, *If you have faith as a mustard seed, you can say to this mulberry tree, 'Be pulled up by the roots and be planted in the sea,' and it would obey you.* (Luke 17:6).

Your faith in God enables you to move forward in His will for your life. God's will for your life unfolds daily as you obey His Word by walking in faith.

> *So then faith comes by hearing, and hearing by the word of God. (Romans 10:17).*

As you hear, listen to, respond to, and obey the Word from God then your faith is quickened, and provides access to all the things God has for you. He provides, protects, and preserves those who place their faith in Him.

> *Trust in the Lord, and do good; Dwell in the land, and feed on His faithfulness.* (Psalm 37:3)

Let me close this chapter on the access to God that is available through our faith with three exhortations. First, keep looking upward in faith to God.

> *I will lift up my eyes to the hills—From whence comes my help? My help comes from the Lord, Who made heaven and earth.* (Psalm 121:1-2)

Lift your eyes past the hill to the One who owns the hill. Like Moses, don't focus on the Egyptians or the sea, focus on God. Keep looking upward in faith to God. Look past difficulties, discouragement, and detours to the One who is the creator and sustainer of life.

Second, keep moving forward with faith in God. The people complained, *We might as well have died in Egypt...*" but faith kept them moving. Faith is not about what you see, but about God's presence, path, and power. In fact, when it seems that you are in an impossible situation, faith is the only thing that can keep you moving. Without faith it is likely you will die in Egypt.

Finally, keep trusting in God's presence, path, promises, and power.

The Lord is my light and my salvation; Whom shall I fear? The Lord is the strength of my life; Of whom shall I be afraid? ...I would have lost heart, unless I had believed That I would see the goodness of the Lord In the land of the living. (Psalm 27:1,13)

Where God leads, He provides, protects, and preserves. He provided for the children in the wilderness, protected them as they crossed the sea, and preserved them for 40 years in the wilderness. The only reason some didn't get into the Promised Land is because they did not have faith. He gave manna from heaven, water, clothes that did not wear out, and they even wore the same shoes for decades. Faith in God is powerful.

Faith is the foundation for our trust in the Lord. You can at all times access God's presence by faith. When it feels like you are between that rock and the hard place, the only way out is through faith. Read His Word, speak to Him in prayer, and follow the path of godly leaders. These are the things that strengthen our faith.

You began your journey with God by faith when you trusted the Lord Jesus to be your Savior. The journey will continue, because that same faith provides access to God, and everything you need.

Chapter 4

The Purposeful Power of Faith

I remain confident of this:
I will see the goodness of the Lord
in the land of the living.
Wait for the Lord;
be strong and take heart
and wait for the Lord. (Psalm 27:13-14)

Waiting is one of the most difficult tasks we face. Nobody likes to wait, and we go to great lengths to avoid the possibility. The medical clinic used to be a place where you always expected to wait. Now, many doctors allow you to check in online and they will call you when it is time to come in.

We purchase movie tickets on our smart phones so we don't have to stand in line at the box office. No doubt, you have seen people enter a busy restaurant, and when they discover it is a 40 minute wait, they leave to find a restaurant where it is only a 30 minute wait.

One of the causes of serious debt problems is created by our inability to wait. People can't wait to get their hands on a desired item, and why should they when it is available with easy credit.

Young people can't wait for marriage before living together, or even purchasing a house together. Waiting for commitment seems so old fashion and unnecessary when you can have it now.

It seems that everyone has a phone or laptop that keeps them entertained if they should ever have to wait for anything. I think it is accurate to say that we have lost the ability to wait.

The truth is that it has never been easy to wait. When Jesus asked the Disciples to wait for him while He went to pray in the garden, they fell asleep (see Matthew 26:36-46). Abraham could not wait for God to provide a son through his wife Sara, so he took matters in his own hands (see Genesis 16:1-4). Saul grew impatient while waiting for Samuel, so he performed the priestly functions himself (see 1 Samuel 13:8-10).

Psalm 27, is a Psalm of David; a Psalm of faith that expresses the necessity of having faith in God. David says he would have lost heart unless he had faith in God. It is important to notice that his faith was not that he would see the pearly gates of glory in the sweet by and by, but that he would see the goodness of the Lord in the land of the living. His faith assured him that he would encounter God's goodness in this life.

To declare that we have placed our faith in God means we believe we will see the goodness of the Lord while we are yet living. Greater things await us, but it is good to know that the power of our faith can lead us to see the goodness of God, in spite of difficult situations. We can, by faith, thank God for the fact that we can see His goodness while we are living.

To declare that we have placed our faith in God means we believe we will see the goodness of the Lord while we are yet living.

The requirement for possessing this kind of faith is waiting. In fact, a key word to describe this passage is patience. If you are anything like me then you were not born with patience. It is something we acquire as we go through life. You have seen times when life seems to have been unwrapped. These are the times when there is nothing you can do but pray to God, and wait upon Him in faith. As you pray to Him, you have to wait.

There is a song that says, *God is an on time God*. He may not come when you want Him, but He is always on time. We sing it, but I don't know if we believe it or not. He is always on time. That's the hard part of waiting—having patience. It is to believe God will show up and we will be able to see His goodness while still in the land of the living.

This is why some have difficulty with the Christian life. They believe everything that is good is on the other side. But Jesus said we could have it now.

> ***The thief does not come except to steal, and to kill, and to destroy. I have come that they may have life, and that they may have it more abundantly.*** (John 10:10)

This is the *goodness of the Lord* David spoke of in Psalm 27. He expected to have what Jesus later would call life to the full.

Because he had faith, he could wait for the Lord. We must understand that waiting on the Lord requires faith. Waiting reveals the power of our faith. You have the ability to wait. It's been said, *little faith–little power*. If we just place our faith in Him, we will learn how to wait on the Lord.

Remember when you were a young child, and your mother took you somewhere and told you to wait until she returned. Like any child, you might have gotten bored, or grew a little restless, but it didn't matter. You waited because you knew your mother would come for you. You had faith in what she said, and who she was, so you were able to wait.

This is the kind of faith David speaks of in Psalm 27. It is more than just sitting down and waiting for something to come to you. It doesn't mean just waiting at the house for something to come to you. I learned a long time ago that if you want to see a ship then it is best to go where the water is. We don't just sit and wait for God to do something for us, we go to where He told us to go—that is where we can expect to see Him best.

This kind of waiting requires faith. If we place our faith in Him, and learn as David learned, how to wait on the Lord, we will not sit around but continue to do what we need to do.

The power of our faith in God is revealed through works and service. If we don't have faith we will not do very much because it means we don't believe God will do what He says He will do. Faith will have an effect on the life we live.

> *So then faith comes by hearing, and hearing by the word of God.* (Romans 10:17)

This is possible by continually hearing and putting God's Word in you in order to have faith. The more we get into God's Word the more we are strengthened. We are to live by faith not by sight.

In Matthew chapter four, Jesus said to Satan that man does not live by bread alone, but by every word that proceeds from the mouth of God. The Word of God is crucial for life. It is important in order for us to have faith. Faith comes because we rely on His Word. We cannot live by bread alone. *Your Word is a lamp for my feet; a light on my path* (Psalm 119:105). This is how we can step out and follow His Word because it is a lamp and light.

The reason we can follow God's leadership from His Word is because our faith will elevate us above our fears. Faith gives us the patience to wait on His will. Others entice us to follow those fears because it sounds right, *a way that seems right to man but leads to destruction* (Proverbs

14:12). However, as we wait in faith we will discover some amazing truths.

The Power Of Your Faith And The Purpose Of Your Life

God has a purpose for your life. Rick Warren in his best-selling book, *The Purpose Driven Life* reminds us that we were not born by accident; God has a purpose for each life. Our life is not about YOU or ME. It is all about His purpose—for His glory, not our happiness. This helps us understand that we are important in His sight.

> We can choose many things—career, spouse, etc., but one thing we cannot choose—our purpose.

We can choose many things—career, spouse, etc., but one thing we cannot choose—our purpose. It was given to us when we were born. In fact, it is like birth itself. No child ever chooses to be born. Birth is based on the choice of others. The same is true with purpose—it is chosen by God.

Our purpose is based on what God has called us to do.

> *And we know that all things work together for good to those who love God, to those who are the called according to His purpose.* (Romans 8:28)

Everything that happens to us is contributing to His purpose for our life. Perhaps we don't like a particular situation, but we understand it is contributing to our good. It is about God's purpose. All of the pains and sorrows and tears are contributing to our good because God has a purpose for our life.

In Psalm 27, David said, no matter how many enemies I had, I believed I would see the goodness of the Lord while I was living. This goodness of the Lord is not just for when we die. We might not understand everything that is happening to us, or how we get to that point, but faith tells us that we will see the goodness of the Lord *in the land of the living*. Even if we don't understand it, because of our faith we can say, *He has been good.*

My parents frequently said God has been better to us than we have been to ourselves. Our faith allows us to wait long enough through the difficult times in order to see the goodness of the Lord. The truth expressed in Romans 8:28 can only be understood through the eyes of faith.

The Power of Your Faith and the Plans of Your Life

God has a plan for your life. Even when the Israelites were in captivity, speaking through his prophet Jeremiah, God revealed that He had a plan and He was working His plan for them.

> ***For I know the thoughts that I think toward you, says the Lord, thoughts of peace and not of evil, to give you a future and a hope.*** (Jeremiah 29:11)

God said go ahead get married and enjoy life in Babylon for 70 years, because He knew the plans He had for them.

Thus says the Lord of hosts, the God of Israel, to all who were carried away captive, whom I have caused to be carried away from Jerusalem to Babylon: Build houses and dwell in them; plant gardens and eat their fruit. Take wives and beget sons and daughters; and take wives for your sons and give your daughters to husbands, so that they may bear sons and daughters—that you may be increased there, and not diminished. And seek the peace of the city where I have caused you to be carried away captive, and pray to the Lord for it; for in its peace you will have peace. (Jeremiah 29:4-7)

Earlier, God said to Jeremiah that he had a plan for him even before he was born (see Jeremiah 1: 5). God said *I knew you before you were born*. That is awesome to think about. Whatever county you were born in, God knew you. He had plans for your life. If you are down, this should pick you up. He knew us even before we were in our mother's womb.

God has already set us apart for the work we do. We might be late getting to the work, but God doesn't give up on us. He allows a little rain, thunder, and lightning, and we get in a hurry, not realizing that He has plans for our lives.

Sometimes God's plan sounds foolish to us. For example, when I stand to preach, it seems foolish that I should open the Bible and talk to people about the Word of God in order to change their lives. But the truth is that God chose this activity to change the world.

For since, in the wisdom of God, the world through wisdom did not know God, it pleased God through the foolishness of the message preached to save those who believe. (1 Corinthians 1:21)

We should be glad that we serve a good and gracious God. We don't have to wait for someone to tell us what we need to do. Before we were born, God had plans for our lives. The power of faith allows us to wait on Him to accomplish His plan. Faith gives us the ability to believe, with David, that we can still see the goodness of the Lord. *Wait on the Lord, but be of good courage, the Lord shall strengthen your heart.* (Psalm 27:14) Don't wait for the letter carrier, or for someone else to do something for you-just wait for the Lord.

The Power of Your Faith and the Priorities of Your Life

> *...seek first the kingdom of God and His righteousness, and all these things shall be added to you.* (Matthew6:33)

Not only does God have a plan for you, He also has priorities for your life. He has prioritized things for us. Seek first His kingdom and all other things (cars, houses, etc.) He will be able to provide for you. Sometimes we get our priorities mixed up. We must understand God is a God of order. When we get mixed up, we seek everything but God.

In the Book of Exodus, we see God's priorities listed for us (chapter 20 lists the Ten Commandments). He told Moses this is what I want you to write—you should have no gods before me, and then down the line. If God is not first, then murder, lying, and stealing will not make a difference. If He is first then everything will fall into place.

We should be glad that He is a God of order. In the beginning He created the heavens and earth. Then He made man in His own image, and gave man a purpose, to be fruitful and multiply. Anything that is not fruitful is not a priority for God. God's priorities will not submit to our priorities.

My personal prayer is that my priorities will follow this progression: *Heavenly Father, help me to be the Christian man, husband, father, father-in-law, grandfather, pastor and the Christian citizen You want me to be.*

David the Psalmist not only wrote the truth, but he also lived the truth. There was a time when David was on the run. King Saul was in pursuit in order to put David to death. It had already been revealed to David that he was to be the next king so you would expect him to grab the first opportunity to seize the throne.

Such an opportunity presented itself. David and his men were hiding in a cave when Saul entered the cave to relieve himself. David's men saw this as an opportunity, and encouraged David to kill the king and assume the throne. Even though he knew God was going to make him king someday, David refused to run ahead of God. Instead, he spared Saul's life. Notice what Saul said when he realized what David had done:

> ***For if a man finds his enemy, will he let him get away safely? Therefore may the Lord reward you with good for what you have done to me this day.*** (1 Samuel 24:19)

Both Saul and David expected the goodness of the Lord to be a reality in their life, not at some point in the future world.

David knew the power of waiting. He was a great man of faith. When he wrote the words of Psalm 27 he was simply sharing a testimony of his own experience. Your faith will also allow you to expect, experience, express, and extend the goodness of the Lord in the land of the living.

> *And behold, there was a man in Jerusalem whose name was Simeon, and this man was just and devout, waiting for the Consolation of Israel, and the Holy Spirit was upon him. And it had been revealed to him by the Holy Spirit that he would not see death before he had seen the Lord's Christ. So he came by the Spirit into the temple. And when the parents brought in the Child Jesus, to do for Him according to the custom of the law, he took Him up in his arms and blessed God...* (Luke 2:25-28)

This man Simeon was very much a man of faith like David. He is described as righteous and devout, one obviously seeking to please God with the way he lived. We are told that he was *looking for the consolation of Israel*. In other words, he was waiting for the salvation God had promised his people. Specifically, Simeon had been told by God's Spirit that he would not die before seeing the Savior. He waited by faith, believing he would see the goodness of the Lord in the land of the living.

Sure enough, his wait was certainly not in vain. When he saw the infant Savior, he knew that he was literally staring at the goodness of the Lord.

Chapter 5

The Participating Power of Faith

Therefore we also, since we are surrounded by so great a cloud of witnesses, let us lay aside every weight, and the sin which so easily ensnares us, and let us run with endurance the race that is set before us, looking unto Jesus, the author and finisher of our faith, who for the joy that was set before Him endured the cross, despising the shame, and has sat down at the right hand of the throne of God. (Hebrews 12:1-2)

What does it profit, my brethren, if someone says he has faith but does not have works? Can faith save him? If a brother or sister is naked and destitute of daily food, and one of you says to them, "Depart in peace, be warmed and filled," but you do not give them the things which are needed for the body, what does it profit? Thus also faith by itself, if it does not have works, is dead.

But someone will say, "You have faith, and I have works." Show me your faith without your works, and I will show you my faith by my works. You believe that there is one God. You do well. Even the demons believe—and tremble! But do you want to know, O foolish man, that faith without works is dead? Was not Abraham our father justified by works when he offered Isaac his son on the altar?

Do you see that faith was working together with his works, and by works faith was made perfect? And the Scripture was fulfilled which says, "Abraham believed God, and it was accounted to him for righteousness." And he was called the friend of God.

You see then that a man is justified by works, and not by faith only. Likewise, was not Rahab the harlot also justified by works when she received the messengers and sent them out another way? For as the body without the spirit is dead, so faith without works is dead also. (James 2:14-26)

If you are close to my age you remember having gym class at school, or perhaps they called it PE at your school. It was 45 minutes to an hour set aside each day to make sure we got plenty of physical exercise. It seems today there is not enough time in the day for such activity.

Usually, one of the requirements of gym class was that we had to run a race. It might have been a short race like a one hundred yard dash, or perhaps half a lap around the track, or maybe even a complete lap. The point is that we all had to be in the race. There were no exceptions if you wanted to pass the class. It didn't matter if you were fast or slow, the only thing that counted was running the race.

In a similar fashion, God has a race for each of us to run. It is a race that varies in length and intensity for each of us, but we must all run the race. Some refer to it as the race of life, but when God created us and put us in this world, He entered us into a race.

The power of your faith in God will keep you in the race of life that is set by God. The race of life is a race that is run by faith in God. In other words, it is a *faith race*. No matter how much you prepare for the race, the preparation will not count unless you enter the race. Therefore, the power of your faith in God empowers and sustains you in the race.

The writer of Hebrews mentions many others who ran the race. They are listed as examples of what it means to run the race of faith. It is the same race we are called to run. One of the best resources we have is others who can provide witness of their race.

The discussion draws in on this cloud of witnesses (Hebrews 12:1-2). Are they the ones who have gone on that we have talked about in Hebrews 11? Are they in heaven looking on us as spectators? Perhaps they are pulling for us to be able to run the race God has set before us as they have done in the past.

They are encouragers for us. We can look back and see the faith of those who loved God and moved out by His word. They bear witness to what it means to run the race. As you know, someone who has been there and done that already is a powerful resource to learn how to do it ourselves. We know it can be done, and that it can be done successfully, because we have this great cloud of witnesses.

It is a race that each of us has to run. It is a race that we cannot delegate to someone else. We cannot say our mother or father ran this race therefore I'm qualified. We cannot depend on the work of anyone else; each person has to run their own race.

The history of the Bible reveals how people entered the race differently. Abram left home and entered the race. Jonah entered the race by running in the wrong direction, both spiritually and physically, yet God used a great fish to change his direction, again both spiritually and physically.

It is also evident that each person enters at a different time. As we have already seen, Abram entered as an old man. Joseph entered as a young man. It doesn't matter when or how we enter, it is still a race. It is the race of faith. The race God allows us to run.

We enter the race through salvation, by grace.

> *For by grace you have been saved through faith, and that not of yourselves; it is the gift of God, not of works, lest anyone should boast. (Ephesians 2:8-9)*

Faith is given to us by God. If you have not trusted Jesus as Savior you are not in the race. You might be in the rat race, but not the faith race. This race is entered by faith.

Not only does each person have a race that is entered differently, at a different time, but also for a different duration. Some have a short race and others have a long race. However, that does not make any difference; it is God who allows us to get in the race. Some people get to the race very early in life, and some, like the thief on the cross, get in the race very late. But the key is to get in the race.

If you are not in that race, the race of faith, then the best time for you to enter the race is right now.

Some folks are like athletes who only prepare for the race in the gym and on the practice field. But, like an athlete, you need to get in the race. It is not enough just to practice. You do have a race to run.

The writer of Hebrews says that some don't want to get in the race because they must eliminate some things; every weight and burdens that will impede progress. In order to run the race successfully, we must lay aside every weight and sin that easily ensnares us run the race that is set before us.

In order to run the race successfully, we must lay aside every weight and sin that easily ensnares us and run the race that is set before us.

When I ran track, I frequently had weights strapped around my legs. These weights were designed to strengthen my legs and prepare me to run the race. However, to run the race I had to pull them off.

With the Christian race we have to put away some things we have been holding on to. This weight is identified as sin, and refers to the sin that keeps us from running the race of faith. You know the sin; it is the sin that causes you to do the opposite of what God wants you to do.

One of the biblical terms for sin can be translated as *missing the mark*. It refers to an archer who aimed at a bull's eye but missed the entire target. To sin is to miss the target.

You know what target you are missing. Every person knows when they miss the target. You cannot run the race with all these weights hanging on you. These weights (sins) keep you from running the race. You want to get them lifted from you so you can run unhindered.

Faith enables you to be an active participant in the race

God gives us the power to be active participants in the race. Some interpreters say the cloud of witnesses are spectators, like fans at a football game cheering us as we run the race. But in light of the descriptions in Hebrews 11, it is more likely they are witnesses in the sense that they have already run the race. They are witnessing to us that running the race is possible and this is how it is done.

We don't need spectators. In fact, there is really only one spectator and that is God. What we need is active participants, those who get rid of the things that hinder them from running the race. It requires eliminating the sin causing you to fall short and miss the mark that God has set for your life.

At the beginning of this chapter you read a passage from the book of James. It was a discussion about faith and the difference between living faith and dead faith. It is a reminder that faith without works is a dead faith. Allow me to paraphrase: *Faith that does nothing is worth nothing*. We can talk it but it does nothing. We must be an active participant.

James provides this warning that spectators are not in the race. Those who only talk about faith need to actually get on the track and begin running the race. If all you do is talk about it and watch others run the race, then your faith is dead—it has no value. True faith allows us to actually enter the race.

> **We have a race to run, and God has given us the power of faith in Him.**

We have a race to run, and God has given us the power of faith in Him. In other words, we have a race to get in. It is not like being on the sidelines or a Monday morning quarterback. A lot of people are waiting for the Dallas Cowboys game so they can be the coach. They plan to sit on their couch and tell the team what they should be doing. Especially on Monday morning, they will have all the answers and tell what they should have done.

This race of faith does not need any sideline or Monday morning quarterbacks. The participant must get in the race.

The word *race* has something to do with agony. It is not easy to run with endurance. Some give up at the drop of a hat, they cannot keep on running. We must run the race that is *set* before us, with patience and endurance.

> *I returned and saw under the sun that—The race is not to the swift, Nor the battle to the strong, Nor bread to the wise, Nor riches to men of understanding, Nor favor to men of skill; But time and chance happen to them all.* (Ecclesiastes 9:11)

It is important to understand that the race is not given to the fastest runner, nor the battle to the strongest warrior, but the one who is able to endure. We have to endure. We must stay in the race with a steady pace. We must keep moving. You don't have to worry about running someone else's race, just run your race.

Remind yourself that God has set this race before you and the power of your faith in him will enable you to run.

Faith enables you to be a productive participant in the race.

A race is going somewhere, moving toward a finish line. When running with endurance, you are moving toward a goal. Again, you can't be productive in the race just thinking about it. You must get in the race. Many are just discussing the race—when I get everything together, when the kids are grown, when I get settled in my new job, after I'm through having fun, etc. The list of reasons for not being productive is endless. For some, the race might be almost over so don't take a chance standing on the sideline and discussing getting in the race. You might wait too long.

I would get in the race by making sure my relationship with Christ is right.

In my younger days I used to run track. When you run track you have an assigned lane. You have to run in your own lane. If I got in someone else's lane I would be disqualified. Some people can't run their own race because they are trying to get in another's lane. Stay in your own lane, and run your own race. When you get in another's lane you are impeding them. It means they have to watch out for you.

You can only be productive in your own lane. God has marked out a race for each of us and there is no need to run in anyone else's lane.

It is also necessary to run until He says the race is over.

> *Not that I have already attained, or am already perfected; but I press on, that I may lay hold of that for which Christ Jesus has also laid hold of me.* (Philippians 3:12)

Paul knew he was in a race, and he was aware the race was not over. He was committed to *pressing on* until he crossed the finish line. Until we cross the finish line, we have to press on because Jesus has done something for us. He has laid hold of life for us; therefore we are running this race. We have not been perfected yet, but we're on our way. We must run looking unto Jesus, the author and finisher of our faith. He initiated and finishes our faith.

Christ endured the cross so we could have endurance for the race. Sometimes the race gets tough but we must stay in the race. Sometimes it feels like hills are coming quickly, but we must stay in the race. Even if it feels like we are too tired to move on we must stay in the race. The devil will tell you it doesn't make any difference if you quit, look around there is no one else running. But, stay in the race, because you have power in your faith in God.

Do you remember the movie *Forrest Gump*. Remember how Forrest was always running, staying in the race. He ran from one end of the country to the other and then he still kept on running. That is what the race of faith is like. The devil wants to impede our progress by discouraging and distracting us. He will do anything to get us to stop. But, if you keep running, and stay in your own lane you will be able to finish the race.

You can't be effective looking around to see what others are doing or if there are other options. If you look around you will discover that you are running all over the place. You must only look to Jesus, the author and finisher of your faith.

Neither can you run while looking back toward where you have been, what you have left, or even what you have accomplished. The quickest way to get out of your lane is to turn around and look behind you.

In the same way it is not possible to run the race of faith by looking at yourself. You can't run the race if all you can see is yourself. Don't let accomplishments get in the way of the race, and be careful not to be sidetracked talking about what you have done and what you have. It is also dangerous to look to friends and acquaintances. The only way to run the race of faith is to look at Jesus.

Jesus is the pioneer and perfecter of our faith; the beginning and ending of our faith. We must run until He says it is all over. He is the alpha and omega of our faith. Don't listen to other voices telling you that you don't have to run. Jesus is the only voice to listen for in the race.

One day you will hear Him say, *Well done, good and faithful servant... You ran well, stayed in the race, stayed in your lane, ran with lightening flashing, thunder roaring, tornados coming, floods everywhere, and everybody giving up on you. When the enemy got in your way you kept in the race. Well done!!!*

Chapter 6

The Perspective of Faith

If you could extract all of the moisture out of a thick fog, 100 feet high, which covered seven square blocks, you would have enough water to fill a small glass. Yet, such a thick fog has a tremendous influence. Fog can close airports, stop traffic, and even create situations resulting in injury and death. However, if we could see beyond the fog we would see that nothing has changed. The fog really has no effect upon reality but it has a tremendous effect upon our perception of reality.

We often live in a spiritual fog. This means that we allow things (often very inconsequential things) to cloud our perception and paralyze our action. The story recorded in 2 Kings 6 tells how one man had a spiritual fog burned away so his eyes could be opened.

The time is the 9th century BC. The prophet of the time was Elisha, the man who had received a double portion of God's Spirit. He was the prominent spokesman for God in the Northern Kingdom of Israel. His story is recorded in 2 Kings 6:

> *Now the king of Syria was making war against Israel; and he consulted with his servants, saying, "My camp will be in such and such a place."*
>
> *And the man of God sent to the king of Israel, saying, "Beware that you do not pass this place, for the Syrians are coming down there."*
>
> *Then the king of Israel sent someone to the place of which the man of God had told him. Thus he warned him, and he was watchful there, not just once or twice.*
>
> *Therefore the heart of the king of Syria was greatly troubled by this thing; and he called his servants and said to them, "Will you not show me which of us is for the king of Israel?"*
>
> *And one of his servants said, "None, my lord, O king; but Elisha, the prophet who is in Israel, tells the king of Israel the words that you speak in your bedroom."*
>
> *So he said, "Go and see where he is, that I may send and get him." And it was told him, saying, "Surely he is in Dothan."*
>
> *Therefore he sent horses and chariots and a great army there, and they came by night and surrounded the city.*
>
> *And when the servant of the man of God arose early and went out, there was an army, surrounding the city with horses and chariots. And his servant said to him, "Alas, my master! What shall we do?"*
>
> *So he answered, "Do not fear, for those who are with us are more than those who are with them."*

And Elisha prayed, and said, "Lord, I pray, open his eyes that he may see." Then the Lord opened the eyes of the young man, and he saw. And behold, the mountain was full of horses and chariots of fire all around Elisha.

So when the Syrians came down to him, Elisha prayed to the Lord, and said, "Strike this people, I pray, with blindness." And He struck them with blindness according to the word of Elisha.

Now Elisha said to them, "This is not the way, nor is this the city. Follow me, and I will bring you to the man whom you seek." But he led them to Samaria.(2 Kings 6:8-19)

This was a time of war, and God's people were under a serious threat from the king of Aram. It is said that all is fair in love and war, but this is one of those situations where it just does not seem fair. There were no secrets for this threatening king. Everything he said or did was revealed to his enemy.

His problem was not a breakdown in internal security, or a successful espionage ring. It was a seemingly harmless prophet named Elisha. God had given him the ability to know what the king of Aram was going to do, perhaps even before he knew himself. Regardless of the battlefield strategy, Elisha passed the information on to the Israelite commander, and the battle was easily won.

There was only one solution for the king of Aram—he had to locate and silence Elisha. Advance scouts told him that Elisha was in the town of Dothan, so the king sent soldiers with horses and chariots to capture this unusual enemy. Elisha's life was in danger.

Here is God's prophet, surrounded by a hostile army of horses and chariots. The stage is set for this godly man to teach us an important lesson about prayer. Judging by the types of requests that are shared at a typical prayer meeting, most of us turn to prayer when we are in the midst of fear and suffering.

Elisha was no stranger to suffering.

Although he was in a desperate situation, Elisha's prayer is not a desperate prayer. It was a prayer of great faith and it reveals the perspective possessed by a person of faith.

Scripture frequently calls us to pray at all times. We are instructed to *pray without ceasing* (1 Thess. 5:17). The whole of life is to be a symphony of prayer offered to God. However, there are particularly stressful times when we especially need to pray. These times include when we are in the presence of danger.

Elisha's servant was up early in the morning. Upon walking outside, perhaps to view the sunrise, he noticed something more frightening on the horizon. The house was completely surrounded by the army of the enemy. The threat was great and the danger was very real. This is definitely a time to pray.

> *Deliver me from my enemies, O my God; Defend me from those who rise up against me. Deliver me from the workers of iniquity, And save me from bloodthirsty men.*(Psalm 59:1-2)

> *Deliver me, O my God, out of the hand of the wicked, Out of the hand of the unrighteous and cruel man.* (Psalm 71:4)

Deliver me, O Lord, from evil men; Preserve me from violent men... (Psalm 140:1)

Any time that we are aware of our weakness is an appropriate time for prayer. Listen to the cry of Elisha's servant: *Alas, my master! What shall we do?* This servant of Elisha was confronted with his own weakness. He realized there was nothing he could do to resolve the situation. At this point we must learn to pray.

Prayer is not the possession of the strong, rich, and powerful. It does not belong exclusively to the religious and faithful. Prayer is available to all who recognize their need to cry out to an all-loving and all-powerful God who cares. Prayer is a resource of faith.

> If you ever find yourself asking, What shall I do?—the answer is PRAY!

When you are in the presence of danger—pray! When confronted by your weakness—pray! When you are facing illness, financial stress, family difficulties or business—pray! If you ever find yourself asking, *What shall I do?*—the answer is PRAY! That is the perspective that comes from living the life of faith.

Elisha, the great man of faith, made an amazing statement. He told his servant that the army with them is greater than the army of the enemy (v.16). It expresses the confidence he had in God. *Do not fear* is an incredible thing to say under the circumstances. It reminds us of Jesus' words to Jarius.

While He was still speaking, some came from the ruler of the synagogue's house who said, "Your daughter is dead. Why trouble the Teacher any further?" As soon as Jesus heard the word that was spoken, He said to the ruler of the synagogue, "Do not be afraid; only believe." (Mark 5:35-36)

Elisha was able to express such great confidence because of his firm conviction that God is greater than the enemy. In Elisha's eyes, the entire Syrian army could have encircled the house but God has more warriors. This is the perspective of faith.

You are of God, little children, and have overcome them, because He who is in you is greater than he who is in the world. (1 John 4:4)

When Elisha prayed, his prayer was based on his confidence that there was nothing to fear, and his conviction that God was great enough to deliver him.

This kind of faith, the same faith that is available to you and I, is found frequently in scripture. Let me introduce you to three Israelite young men, Shadrach, Meshach, and Abednego who demonstrated this same faith.

Then Nebuchadnezzar, in rage and fury, gave the command to bring Shadrach, Meshach, and Abed-Nego. So they brought these men before the king. Nebuchadnezzar spoke, saying to them, "Is it true, Shadrach, Meshach, and Abed-Nego, that you do not serve my gods or worship the gold image which I have set up? Now if you are ready at the time you hear the sound of the horn, flute, harp, lyre, and psaltery, in symphony with all kinds of music, and you fall down and worship the image which I have made, good! But if you do not worship, you shall be cast immediately into the midst of a burning fiery furnace. And who is the god who will deliver you from my hands?" (Daniel 3:13-15)

The enemy they faced was just as real as the Syrian army surrounding Elisha and his servant. It was just as real as any situation you are facing in your world. We don't have to live long before we find ourselves in a place where it seems impossible. The enemy can be visible or invisible, but it is just as real.

Now, listen to the response of these three young men.

Shadrach, Meshach, and Abed-Nego answered and said to the king, "O Nebuchadnezzar, we have no need to answer you in this matter. If that is the case, our God whom we serve is able to deliver us from the burning fiery furnace, and He will deliver us from your hand, O king. But if not, let it be known to you, O king, that we do not serve your gods, nor will we worship the gold image which you have set up." (Daniel 3:16-18)

Do you hear their testimony of faith? They said, *We're not worried about it. Even if you do throw us in the furnace God is able to deliver us.* That is a marvelous testimony about their confidence in God. Do you believe God is able to deliver you from your situation? That is what it means to live the life of faith.

But, it gets even better. They continued their statement of faith: *But even if he does not, we want you to know... that we will not serve your gods or worship the image of gold you have set up.* Wow! That is some kind of faith. They believed God would take care of them, but even if He didn't for some reason, it didn't matter, they were going to continue in the race. That is truly the perspective of faith.

So, what happened to the three men of faith?

> *Then Nebuchadnezzar was full of fury, and the expression on his face changed toward Shadrach, Meshach, and Abed-Nego. He spoke and commanded that they heat the furnace seven times more than it was usually heated. And he commanded certain mighty men of valor who were in his army to bind Shadrach, Meshach, and Abed-Nego, and cast them into the burning fiery furnace.*
>
> *Then King Nebuchadnezzar was astonished; and he rose in haste and spoke, saying to his counselors, "Did we not cast three men bound into the midst of the fire?" They answered and said to the king, "True, O king."*
>
> *"Look!" he answered, "I see four men loose, walking in the midst of the fire; and they are not hurt, and the form of the fourth is like the Son of God."*
>
> *Then Nebuchadnezzar went near the mouth of the burning fiery furnace and spoke, saying, "Shadrach, Meshach, and Abed-Nego, servants of the Most High God, come out, and come here." Then Shadrach, Meshach, and Abed-Nego came from the midst of the fire.* (Daniel 3:19-20, 24-26)

The king was angry, kept his word, heated the fire, and threw them in the furnace. There they walked around until God led them out. God provided! Their faith was proven valid. It is the right thing to do to trust in God completely, even when things seem impossible.

Faith looks at life from a different perspective. Instead of seeing blazing furnaces, insurmountable mountains, impenetrable problems, and defeating despair, faith sees God and His ability to meet our every need. Because they had the same faith as Elisha they shared the same perspective.

Returning to our friend Elisha, there are some things about faith that we can learn from his prayer. First, note that he did not pray for victory or deliverance. Why? Because deliverance was already available. God's army was already present, victory was assured. There was no need to seek God's intervention. How much of our praying is simply begging God for victory (ie. illness, problems, finances, etc.). God had already won the victory.

> ***These things I have spoken to you, that in Me you may have peace. In the world you will have tribulation; but be of good cheer, I have overcome the world."*** (John 16:33)

The phrase *I have overcome* is in the verb tense which indicates completed action. Faith is not based on a hope that something happens, but on the reality that God is in control.

> Faith is not based on a hope that something happens, but on the reality that God is in control.

Elisha's prayer was very simple, *Open his eyes...* He prayed that his servant would be able to see reality. God's army was already available. Victory was achieved, but the servant needed to see the victory.

President Harry Truman once said that *we have nothing to fear but fear itself*. We are always afraid of the unknown. A child fears what might be in the dark. We fear new situations and places, of what to expect. We fear death because we have never been there before.

Elisha's servant was afraid because of his blindness, he could not see everything that was real. Elisha was the kind of man who could have prayed for God to lift them out of the situation. Instead, he prayed to see what God was doing. He asked to see the spiritual reality rather than change the physical reality.

We should frequently pray, *Lord, let me see what you are doing*. It is the prayer of one who has the correct perspective of faith.

The prayer of Elisha proved effective in several ways. *The Lord opened his eyes....and he saw*. No longer did he see the horses and chariots of the enemy, but he saw the army of God. Instead of man's perspective, he now saw reality from God's perspective (see Psalm 121).

The prayer also provided concrete benefits. It brought actual deliverance from the hostile army. Note the contrast between the servant who received spiritual vision and the Syrian army which experienced physical blindness.

The Syrian army was not just a threat to Elisha and his servant. They were the enemy of all of Israel. Elisha led the blind army into the capital city and the entire nation benefited from this prayer.

Perhaps you have heard the testimony of someone who was blind at one time, but through surgical techniques they had their vision restored. These people will testify how being able to see touches and affects virtually every aspect of their lives.

When God opens our spiritual eyes, and we see from the correct perspective of faith, it will affect every area of our lives. It is like the sun coming out from behind the clouds, we see things in a new light, with new warmth, and new understanding.

If you find it difficult to look at life from the perspective of faith, perhaps you should seek what the blind man sought from Jesus.

> *Now they came to Jericho. As He went out of Jericho with His disciples and a great multitude, blind Bartimaeus, the son of Timaeus, sat by the road begging. And when he heard that it was Jesus of Nazareth, he began to cry out and say, "Jesus, Son of David, have mercy on me!"*
>
> *Then many warned him to be quiet; but he cried out all the more, "Son of David, have mercy on me!"*
>
> *So Jesus stood still and commanded him to be called. Then they called the blind man, saying to him, "Be of good cheer. Rise, He is calling you."*
>
> *And throwing aside his garment, he rose and came to Jesus. So Jesus answered and said to him, "What do you want Me to do for you?" The blind man said to Him, "Rabboni, that I may receive my sight."*
>
> *Then Jesus said to him, "Go your way; your faith has made you well." And immediately he received his sight and followed Jesus on the road.* (Mark 10:46-52)

When Jesus asked what he wanted, he replied, *I want to see.*

Chapter Seven

The Proving Power of Faith

Now it came to pass after these things that God tested Abraham, and said to him, "Abraham!" And he said, "Here I am."

Then He said, "Take now your son, your only son Isaac, whom you love, and go to the land of Moriah, and offer him there as a burnt offering on one of the mountains of which I shall tell you."

So Abraham rose early in the morning and saddled his donkey, and took two of his young men with him, and Isaac his son; and he split the wood for the burnt offering, and arose and went to the place of which God had told him.

Then on the third day Abraham lifted his eyes and saw the place afar off.

And Abraham said to his young men, "Stay here with the donkey; the lad and I will go yonder and worship, and we will come back to you."

So Abraham took the wood of the burnt offering and laid it on Isaac his son; and he took the fire in his hand, and a knife, and the two of them went together.

But Isaac spoke to Abraham his father and said, "My father!" And he said, "Here I am, my son." Then he said, "Look, the fire and the wood, but where is the lamb for a burnt offering?"

And Abraham said, "My son, God will provide for Himself the lamb for a burnt offering." So the two of them went together. (Genesis 22:1-8)

Any parent who has read the twenty-second chapter of Genesis understands the amazing act of faith demonstrated by Abraham. The ability to say yes to God when it required such an enormous cost is not easy for anyone. In fact, it is hard to comprehend how anyone could possess such a powerful faith.

How can you know the power of your faith in God? There is no way of knowing the power of your faith in God unless your faith has been tested. Perhaps your faith was tested through a job change, or job loss, or layoff. Your faith could have been tested through betrayal of a good friend. As a student, your faith in God could have been tested through your decision to play a sport and the conditioning was difficult, but you didn't quit. Your faith in God as a Christian caused you to believe you could make it, and you did.

Our faith causes us to believe that we can make it. Sometimes all you have is your faith in God. You realize quickly the power of your faith in God when things are not going the way you would like.

When our faith is tested, it is not for the purpose of tripping us up, but to allow us to know the strength of our faith when it is placed in God. We place our faith in that which we do not see, but what we are hoping for. Faith enables us to keep moving forward. It is about the future.

God made a promise to Abram, but first called him to a land unknown. It was through Isaac that the earth would receive blessings, and then God gave Abram a test that would require the sacrifice of his son. We are not to focus on the test, but the faith he had. Abram somehow believed that no matter what he did, God would raise up his son, even if he offered him as a sacrifice.

As you read the story, you can understand the curiosity of Isaac. He had seen it play out many times. He knew if you had the wood and fire then there needed to be a sacrifice. So he asked his father what they were going to offer.

When Abraham came to the place God directed him, he left servants behind and said, *We will come back to you.* This is what faith is about.

> ***By faith Abraham, when he was tested, offered up Isaac, and he who had received the promises offered up his only begotten son, of whom it was said, "In Isaac your seed shall be called," concluding that God was able to raise him up, even from the dead, from which he also received him in a figurative sense.*** (Hebrews 11:17-19)

Even in testing of his faith Abraham trusted in God.

He said to his son, *God will provide for himself the lamb for a burnt offering*. So the two of them went off together; the boy trusting his father and the father trusting God. In a sense, they were both walking in faith.

Abraham demonstrates that the power of faith rests in our belief in the Word of God.

> ***For the word of God is living and powerful, and sharper than any two-edged sword, piercing even to the division of soul and spirit, and of joints and marrow, and is a discerner of the thoughts and intents of the heart.*** (Hebrews 4:12)

The Word of God is powerful, and our faith is powerful when it is in the living and powerful Word. When Jesus was tempted (see Matthew 4) He said, *It is written...* in response to the tests. It is God's Word and when you and I face tests we must remember *it is written*. It is the Word of God.

> ***So then faith comes by hearing, and hearing by the word of God.*** (Romans 10:17)

We must place our faith in the Word of God, not in what someone is saying. We can look at God's Word and see what God has to say to us.

Abraham knew that God himself would provide the lamb. By faith he obeyed God. He placed his faith and trust in God. Faith is a power to live with, and also a power to die in. Those of faith listed in Hebrews 11 did not see the power of God, but knew it was in the future.

There is no other way to live. We cannot live by sight. We have to live by faith. No matter what it looks like we will take our stand on the Word of God. It allows us to follow the example Abraham set. He believed God.

> ***And he believed in the Lord, and He accounted it to him for righteousness.*** (Genesis 15:6)

Because he believed God, God put it in his account. Not because God owed him anything, but because he believed.

Your faith has also been tested and you withstood the test. Therefore, the power of your faith in God enabled you to keep moving forward. Now the next time you encounter a difficult situation you will remember how your faith in God enabled you to withstand your previous test.

This is what Genesis 22 is about. Abraham's faith in God enabled him to withstand a difficult test in obeying God's command of offering up his son Isaac as a burnt sacrifice on one of the mountains which God would show him. The power of your faith in God causes you to believe in the promises of God. When we say that we have faith in God it means that we believe that God will fulfill His promises found in the Bible.

The power of your faith in God is revealed through your decisions and choices. Abraham chose to obey God. We read of Abraham's faith in the book of the Hebrews, *By faith Abraham obeyed when he was called to go out to the place which he would receive as an inheritance and he went out, not knowing where he was going.* (Hebrews 11:8)

Abraham's faith is a prime example of the power of one's faith in God. The power of one's faith in God is a power to live with as well as a power to die in. *These all died in faith, not having received the promises, but having seen them afar off were assured of them, embraced them and confessed that they were strangers and pilgrims on the earth.*

Abraham's Faith was in the Promises of God

Earlier in the book of Genesis, God established a covenant (a promise) with Abraham. He said he was going to bless him (see Genesis 15). When Abraham looked at the sky he believed in the Lord. Abram's name was changed at that moment and he became Abraham. God was in the process of making him a father, one who was exceedingly fruitful. In fact, God promised to bless all the nations through Abraham as kings would come from his lineage. These promises of God led us to Abraham's great test. The test was given to prove, to demonstrate that Abraham believed God's Word.

In Genesis 18, God gave him and Sarah a son, even though they were both well past the childbearing age. God kept His word. Even though Abraham and Sarah were nearly a century old God gave them a son. This was the foundation of Abraham's faith—confidence that God would keep His Word.

He knew that God's promises would never fail. The Bible says, *Blessed be the Lord, who has given rest to His people Israel, according to all that He promised. There has not failed one word of all His good promise, which He promised through*

His servant Moses. (1 Kings 8:56). Moses, another great man of faith, knew that God would keep His Word.

> ***Therefore it is of faith that it might be according to grace, so that the promise might be sure to all the seed, not only to those who are of the law, but also to those who are of the faith of Abraham, who is the father of us all.*** (Romans 4:16)

God's promises are good for all of us. No matter how life is going we must put our faith in the promises of God. If we put our faith in His promises we are assured of success, of things working out, maybe not according to the way we want, but according to His plan.

Abraham's Faith was in the Power of God

Abraham believed in the power of God. Earlier when he and Sarah learned they were to have a child in their old age they both struggled with the news. The angel of God assured them that such was the case and then posed this rhetorical question—*Is anything too hard for the Lord? I will return to you at the appointed time next year, and Sarah will have a son.* (Genesis 18:14)

Over the next few years, Abraham would learn the truth of those words—nothing is too hard for God. He is the creator and sustainer of the universe. The wind and the sea obey Him. There is nothing He cannot do. I wonder sometimes why we ever question God's ability to do something that He has promised. If He truly is God then nothing can stand in His way.

To have faith means that we rest in His power. Abraham placed his faith in the power of God. When things are falling apart we must place our faith in the power of God. There is nothing that can happen to us that is too difficult for God. Yet it might be too difficult for me, or it might be too difficult for others, but not for God. We serve an able God. Nothing is too hard for Him. If God can create the heavens and earth, if He can speak and they come into being, then certainly nothing is too difficult.

> All of the great women and men of faith listed in Hebrews 11 faced situations and circumstances as difficult as anything we face.

If creation is not too hard then the circumstances we face are not too hard for God. All of the great women and men of faith listed in Hebrews 11 faced situations and circumstances as difficult as anything we face.

Noah stood in the midst of a hostile crowd and constructed an enormous ark, even at a time when it had never rained before. Abraham set out from his home to a land he knew nothing about and lived in tents in his quest to follow God. Joseph was left to die in the depths of an Egyptian dungeon. Moses stood before the most powerful man in the world and demanded that he release God's people. On and on the list goes, describing men and women who had faith in the power of God. The same faith is available to you and I today. The faith that will allow us to do the things God has called us to do.

Abraham's Faith was in the Provisions of God

Abraham assured Isaac as they walked up the mountainside that God will provide the lamb. It was a faith moment as they walked side by side. It was an opportunity for a father to teach his son how to trust in God. We must place our faith in God.

Psalm 24:1 reminds us that His provisions are unlimited because He owns everything. Abraham said I don't know how but I have this faith that God will provide. He provided when I left my father and mother looking for the land. He provided Isaac to Sarah and me in our old age. We must believe that God will provide.

> *And my God shall supply all your need according to His riches in glory by Christ Jesus.* (Philippians 4:19)

Abraham needed God to provide. God provided! Abraham lifted his eyes and saw the ram caught in a thicket, and he offered it instead of his son.

If God is able to provide for Abraham he is able to provide for us. As a reminder of God's provision, Abraham called the name of the place *The Lord will Provide*.

When we come up against a wall in our lives that seems like the end of the road, we can say one thing—the Lord will provide. Even when things are not working out like we want, we can truly say with Abraham—the Lord will provide. Faith allows us to keep a positive attitude when the road gets rough, the mountains get high, and the valleys get low. We don't know how, when, or where, but we know the Lord will provide.

In verse 19 we are told that Abraham believed that God would raise Isaac from the dead, if necessary. That is an amazing and incomprehensible expression of faith. You see, everything that God had promised to him was wrapped up in the life of Isaac. Abraham was willing to give up his son in obedience to God, confident that God would still find a way to fulfill His promise.

When you don't see your way out of a situation, place your faith in the Lord. He is not a god who has been made with hands. He is the God who is alive; therefore we put our trust in Him, no matter what is going on around us. *Trust in the Lord with all your heart, And lean not on your own understanding; In all your ways acknowledge Him, And He shall direct your paths.* (Proverbs 3:5-6)

The provision of a goat in a nearby thicket is a great picture of what God has done for us in His son Jesus. John the Baptist recognized it when he said, *Behold the lamb of God...* as he pointed to Jesus. Jesus came to die for our sins. Through Jesus, He has provided salvation for the lost. God also provided His Son Jesus as the sacrifice for the sins of the world.

> *For God so loved the world that He gave His only begotten Son, that whoever believes in Him should not perish but have everlasting life.* (John 3:16)

Chapter 8

The Secret to Walking by Faith

...we walk by faith, not by sight. (2 Corinthians 5:7)

In describing himself before meeting Jesus, the Apostle Paul essentially said he was an ardent defender of the Jewish faith as understood by the sect known as Pharisees. You remember the Pharisees as the ones who gave Jesus the most difficulty, criticizing His every move and teaching. Paul fit right in with them, even describing himself as a *Pharisee of the Pharisees.* In other words, he was as good as it gets.

But something happened, and Paul went from being Jesus' most harsh opponent to His most passionate defender. He had an experience that transformed his life within a very short period of time. Instead of seeking out and punishing followers of Jesus he became a zealous missionary for the Christian faith.

If I were to sum up the transformation with a concise phrase, I would say that Paul was struck blind. Remember how Paul, armed with weapons and ruthless associates, was cutting a swath on the road toward Damascus, hoping to root out Christians (see Acts 9). Along the way, God appeared to Saul (this was Paul's name before he met Jesus), and through a startling voice from heaven and a vision he met Jesus for the first time. As a result he was struck blind, requiring helpers to lead him by hand from place to place.

> Once we begin making decisions based on what we can see, or detect with any of our other senses, then we are not walking in faith.

However, the blindness only lasted a few short days, and God restored his vision. But, from that moment on, Paul became one of the greatest preachers and missionaries in the history of the church. If you consider all of his writings, it is probably accurate to say that Paul has influenced more people for Jesus than any other person in history.

The man who found Jesus because of blindness wrote the words recorded at the beginning of this chapter—*we walk by faith, not by sight*. Certainly it was not simply the few days of blindness that informed Paul, but the whole of his experience. He knew that sight can be deceiving and incomplete. In order to live in the power that God has for us, we must learn to live in faith, not sight.

The secret of walking by faith is to not be limited by our sight. Once we begin making decisions based on what we can see, or detect with any of our other senses, then we are not walking in faith.

Perhaps it is time to pause and look back at what we have already learned. Faith is the *substance of things hoped for* and also the *evidence of things not seen*. We walk by faith when we walk according to the Word of God.

> *So then faith comes by hearing, and hearing by the word of God.* (Romans 10:17)

Therefore, the secret to walking by faith is to walk according to God's Word.

There is a great illustration of this truth found in a fascinating story about God's prophet Elijah. He had been living for some time in the wilderness, completely dependent upon God's daily provisions of life's necessities. We pick up the story when God spoke to him and told him it was time to move on—more lessons to learn.

> *Then the word of the Lord came to him: "Go at once to Zarephath in the region of Sidon and stay there. I have directed a widow there to supply you with food."*
>
> *So he went to Zarephath. When he came to the town gate, a widow was there gathering sticks. He called to her and asked, "Would you bring me a little water in a jar so I may have a drink?"*
>
> *As she was going to get it, he called, "And bring me, please, a piece of bread."*

"As surely as the Lord your God lives," she replied, "I don't have any bread—only a handful of flour in a jar and a little olive oil in a jug. I am gathering a few sticks to take home and make a meal for myself and my son, that we may eat it—and die."

Elijah said to her, "Don't be afraid. Go home and do as you have said. But first make a small loaf of bread for me from what you have and bring it to me, and then make something for yourself and your son. For this is what the Lord, the God of Israel, says: 'The jar of flour will not be used up and the jug of oil will not run dry until the day the Lord sends rain on the land.'"

She went away and did as Elijah had told her. So there was food every day for Elijah and for the woman and her family. For the jar of flour was not used up and the jug of oil did not run dry, in keeping with the word of the Lord spoken by Elijah. (1 Kings 17:8-15)

The land was in the midst of a famine, and this poverty stricken woman and her son were down to their last meal—literally. As a widow in Old Testament times, we know she had no means of her own. She was completely dependent upon the kindness of others. Elijah showed up and informed her that God wanted her to provide a meal for the prophet.

We read these stories sometimes without stopping to reflect on the enormity of the events. Put yourself in this woman's shoes. You have barely enough food for your son and perhaps a few spare bites for yourself. A prophet of God shows up to tell you that you are supposed to give him the food, but don't worry about it, God will provide for you.

What are you going to do? Your first reaction is probably to tell this man to get lost, or if you are going to be a little more polite you might apologetically say that you can't help him. But, then the prophet speaks a word on behalf of God. He promised that if she obeyed she would have enough flour and oil until the drought ends.

At that moment she was confronted with an option. She could either continue on with her plan to prepare a final meal for herself and her son in hopes to buy enough time for something to happen, or she could put her faith in this unusual request and word from God's spokesman. The promise was that if she would step out and walk according to faith then she would be blessed. In other words, she was being asked to walk by faith and not by sight.

This book is about the power of your faith. It is a power that can only be experienced by those who are living, or walking by faith.

This woman took the challenge and did as Elijah instructed. She chose to live by faith.

> *The steps of a good man are ordered by the Lord, And He delights in his way.* (Psalm 37:23)

This book is about the power of your faith. It is a power that can only be experienced by those who are living, or walking by faith. Consequently, I want to share three great truths you will need to know if you choose the life of faith.

First Truth: Get Active

When Paul reminded us that we *walk by faith* he used a term that carries the idea of action and movement. It is the word a writer would use to describe someone walking from point A to point B. It means to get on your feet and use your legs to move. The implication for us is that the life of faith does not come to those who sit down and wait for it. We must be moving, actively involved in experiencing the life of faith.

It is discouraging to see so many people sitting and praying for God to do something in their life. Don't misunderstand; I am not saying that praying is not necessary or valuable. What I mean is that so many people stop at simply praying. They pray for God to act, and then sit down and wait for the answer.

If you think the walk of faith means doing little more than sitting back and waiting for God to do everything for you then you are seriously mistaken. God is not, nor will He ever be, our servant. He does not give us the promises of faith in order to allow us to have a life of ease and comfort. He gives us faith so that we have the resource to deal with all that life will throw at us.

Life is hard, and it will continue to be hard as long as we are on this side of heaven. Nowhere does God promise, even to the ones with the greatest faith, that they will be spared from the harshness of life. That is what the eleventh chapter of Hebrews is all about. It is a list of the great men and women of faith. We would like it to say that those with faith were lifted above the fray and allowed to rest in peace and quiet. But, instead it speaks of the struggles they endured. There are two great truths evident with every person mentioned in this great roll call of faith. They all suffered and they all endured because of their faith.

They *walked.* That is the secret to the power of faith in your life—you must keep on walking according to the truth of God's Word.

Second Truth: Trust God's Word

All the great Old Testament characters who are examples of walking in faith were known for the trust in the Word of God. By faith, Noah followed God's instructions and built an ark. By faith, Abram heard God's call to move to a foreign land. By faith, Moses' parents hid him for three months according to God's Word. By faith, Moses led the people through the wilderness, following God's miraculous symbols. By faith, the walls of Jericho fell as God's army obediently marched around the city. (Hebrews 11)

The thing that separates faith from mere wishful thinking or hopeful speculation is the Word of God. We don't build our faith on what we hope will happen, or what makes sense in our own eyes. We establish our faith on the sure, revealed Word of God. Otherwise, it is not faith.

The secret to a powerful life of faith is to believe God's Word. All the things you have been taught about reading the Bible, meditating on His Word, memorizing scripture verses, doing in-depth study are all necessary to experience the power of faith. The person who is ignorant of

God's Word is unable to trust in God's Word. Remember, faith comes by hearing the Word of God.

Third Truth: Avoid Distractions

Walking in faith is not easy, often requiring all the effort we can muster. It is not easy to walk according to God's Word when everyone keeps telling us we should be doing something different. Imagine if the woman in our story would have told her neighbors what Elijah had instructed her to do. Do you think they would have said something like, *What a great idea, go ahead and make him the largest loaf of bread you can bake*!

Circumstances often suggest that God's way is not the correct way. Remember, many of the giants of faith listed in Hebrews 11 did not live long enough to see the fulfillment of God's promise, yet they were not distracted.

As you strive to walk in faith, there will definitely be distractions. Plans will fall through, failure might seem apparent, friends and family will question what you are doing, and you might even doubt within yourself. However, the secret to success is not to allow distractions, no matter how imposing, to keep you from following the revealed Word of God.

Learning to pilot an airplane is an exciting adventure for many folks. The first license in the process is a VFR, which stands for Visual Flight Rules. However, if you are serious about flying often, you will obviously want an IFR rating. The IFR license allows the pilot to fly using instruments rather than strictly visual sight.

The reason this is so important is because it is not always a wise thing to trust our eyesight. The obvious situation is being caught in a storm or flying at night when there are no guiding lights. I have been told that the hardest part of flying according to instruments rather than visual sight is learning to trust the instruments. Often, what the instrument records and what our vision sees are not the same.

It is possible that what you think is going upward in reality is going downward. The instruments do not suffer from such delusions. Therefore, the instruments are a more reliable source for guidance.

This is what it is like to *walk by faith, not by sight*. It is like flying a plane with an IFR rating. We must live our lives, not according to what we see and experience with our senses, but according to the Word of God. This doesn't mean we are to be ignorant of the world around us, it simply means we are to take our marching orders from God. That is what it means to have faith.

Chapter 9

Testing Your Faith

My brethren, count it all joy when you fall into various trials, knowing that the testing of your faith produces patience. But let patience have its perfect work, that you may be perfect and complete, lacking nothing. If any of you lacks wisdom, let him ask of God, who gives to all liberally and without reproach, and it will be given to him. But let him ask in faith, with no doubting, for he who doubts is like a wave of the sea driven and tossed by the wind. For let not that man suppose that he will receive anything from the Lord; he is a double-minded man, unstable in all his ways. (James 1:2-8)

After all that we have said about faith, think how amazing it would be to have faith that is *mature and complete, not lacking anything*. At that point we will feel confident that we will join the great heroes of faith listed in the 11th chapter of Hebrews.

The problem is that this kind of faith does not just happen because we say a prayer or wait patiently in a church pew. This faith is the result of persistent growth, relentless refining, and frequent testing. That is why the Book of James begins with the admonition to rejoice in the midst of trials. In fact, it can be said that the entire book of James presents a variety of tests that we face in order to prove our faith.

These tests are designed to produce perseverance or endurance. These tests are like training for an athlete, or practice for a musician. God does not give us tests in order to make us fail, but in order to make us succeed. Note the result of God's testing. First, we will be mature, or the word can be translated *perfect*. It means to be fit for the task.

The second term is *complete*. It has the meaning of not lacking anything we need, and without blemish. To be deficient in nothing means that we have everything we need for victorious living. The tests of God are designed to prepare us to experience the power of faith working in our lives.

Our Attitude Toward God's People

> *My brethren, do not hold the faith of our Lord Jesus Christ, the Lord of glory, with partiality. For if there should come into your assembly a man with gold rings, in fine apparel, and there should also come in a poor man in filthy clothes, and you pay attention to the one wearing the fine clothes and say to him, "You sit here in a good place," and say to the poor man, "You*

> *stand there," or, "Sit here at my footstool," have you not shown partiality among yourselves, and become judges with evil thoughts?*
>
> *Listen, my beloved brethren: Has God not chosen the poor of this world to be rich in faith and heirs of the kingdom which He promised to those who love Him? But you have dishonored the poor man. Do not the rich oppress you and drag you into the courts? Do they not blaspheme that noble name by which you are called?*
>
> *If you really fulfill the royal law according to the Scripture, "You shall love your neighbor as yourself," you do well; but if you show partiality, you commit sin, and are convicted by the law as transgressors. For whoever shall keep the whole law, and yet stumble in one point, he is guilty of all. For He who said, "Do not commit adultery," also said, "Do not murder." Now if you do not commit adultery, but you do murder, you have become a transgressor of the law. So speak and so do as those who will be judged by the law of liberty. For judgment is without mercy to the one who has shown no mercy. Mercy triumphs over judgment.* (James 2:1-13)

It is often said that Christians are the most malicious toward other Christians. We tend to fight over denominational differences, petty theological issues, and insignificant activities. One of the tests of faith before us is how we treat other believers.

Passing this test requires denying personal favoritism toward others. It is tempting to give special privilege to certain types of people simply because of their status. However, James calls us to relate to everyone just as Jesus does. There is no partiality with God (see Romans 2:11).

All of us are sinners saved by God's grace. Anything that we are or will ever be is a result of God's work in our lives. Therefore, we have no cause to consider ourselves God's personal favorites.

In order to help us understand this truth, James provides an example of a wealthy man being given preferential treatment solely because of his money. We are always tempted to pay closer attention to those who have the things we would like to possess. Once we begin to notice the appearance and possessions of others, we will begin to show them partiality.

The appropriate attitude toward all people, especially those different than us, is to show mercy.

The proper approach is to see people as individuals, each possessing special qualities and desirable features. They may not be like us, they may even be lower on the social and economic scale, but they are still individuals loved by God. The appropriate attitude toward all people, especially those different than us, is to show mercy.

This is the great hope that each of us have in Jesus—mercy. Through Jesus, God extends mercy, not judgment. He is not interested in judging our lifestyle and actions; He is concerned with changing us through His mercy. The best way to help another person is not through judgment. Judgment drives people away, but mercy draws them near. Judgment creates barriers, mercy overcomes differences.

Every person you meet can be a test of your faith put before you by God. These tests are not designed to trip us up, but to strengthen our faith.

Our Attitude Toward God's Word

> *Therefore lay aside all filthiness and overflow of wickedness, and receive with meekness the implanted word, which is able to save your souls.*
>
> *But be doers of the word, and not hearers only, deceiving yourselves. For if anyone is a hearer of the word and not a doer, he is like a man observing his natural face in a mirror; for he observes himself, goes away, and immediately forgets what kind of man he was. But he who looks into the perfect law of liberty and continues in it, and is not a forgetful hearer but a doer of the work, this one will be blessed in what he does.* (James 1:21-25)

We have already discussed the importance of God's Word and how it relates to our faith. One of the tests of faith listed by James is our attitude toward His Word. He uses the analogy of undressing or changing clothes. In other words, we must be properly dressed to receive the Word of God, just as a guest would not come to a banquet wearing improper clothes.

He lists the dirty outer garments that must be removed. He refers to filthiness by using a medical term that speaks of *the way into the ear*. It is a reference to the dirt or impurity in the ear that keeps us from hearing the Word.

We must not allow this filthy, earwax-like stuff turn us deaf to God's Word.

Rayland III was the Duke of Belgium in the 14th century. The most memorable thing about Rayland was that he was extremely overweight. His younger brother Edward led a revolt and seized control. He did not want to kill his brother so he placed him in a castle room with doors and windows that were a little smaller than normal. Rayland was free to come and go as he pleased, but Edward kept sending in enormous amounts of food. Rayland ate the food that kept him from being able to fit through the door. For 10 years he stayed as a prisoner to his own appetite.

The test not only applies to our outer actions but to the inner as well. We prepare by getting rid of the excess malice, which describes inner dispositions that lead to outer actions. Obviously, getting rid of the inner is more difficult because we usually keep them secret from others, and often even lie to ourselves. But, in order to adequately receive the Word of God this is a test we must pass.

Now that we have a clearer picture of those things that make our clothes dirty, the natural question is how do we take them off. How can I remove these sins of action and attitude? I have searched the scriptures and tried to develop a simple formula, for example, *Four Steps to Removing Sin*. However, I could not find such a formula. My search was in vain because all I found was words like *lay aside, put away,* or *take off* all these sins. In other words, there is no easy, simple formula to follow. It is simply a deliberate, conscious choice to stop sinning. That is how we pass the test and realize the power of our faith.

Our Attitude toward Works

What does it profit, my brethren, if someone says he has faith but does not have works? Can faith save him? If a brother or sister is naked and destitute of daily food, and one of you says to them, "Depart in peace, be warmed and filled," but you do not give them the things which are needed for the body, what does it profit? Thus also faith by itself, if it does not have works, is dead.

But someone will say, "You have faith, and I have works." Show me your faith without your works, and I will show you my faith by my works. You believe that there is one God. You do well. Even the demons believe—and tremble! But do you want to know, O foolish man, that faith without works is dead? Was not Abraham our father justified by works when he offered Isaac his son on the altar? Do you see that faith was working together with his works, and by works faith was made perfect? And the Scripture was fulfilled which says, "Abraham believed God, and it was accounted to him for righteousness." And he was called the friend of God. You see then that a man is justified by works, and not by faith only.

Likewise, was not Rahab the harlot also justified by works when she received the messengers and sent them out another way?

For as the body without the spirit is dead, so faith without works is dead also. (James 2:14-26)

No one can be saved by works; but equally true that no one can be saved without producing works. We are not saved by deeds; we are saved for deeds. Faith, as it is commonly used in the New Testament, means the commitment of one's life, without reservation, to God in Jesus

Christ. All other types of faith are weak and inadequate. Faith that does not show itself cannot save.

Faith that is shown only by profession and not by action is without value, and has no power to help others, or to save the one who professes the faith. Verse 18 reminds us that faith and works are not an either/or but a both/and. In a well-proportioned life there must be thoughts and actions, prayer and effort, faith and works. No man will ever be moved to action without faith, and no man's faith is real until it moves him to action. Faith and works are opposite sides of man's experience of God.

Abraham *believed in the Lord* (Genesis 15:6), but it was not a dead faith. The opportunity arose for putting it to the test (Genesis 22) when God asked for a sacrifice. His works consisted in his throwing himself upon God, not by what he said but by what he did. He was justified by a faith that works.

The Attitude of Our Tongue

My brethren, let not many of you become teachers, knowing that we shall receive a stricter judgment. For we all stumble in many things. If anyone does not stumble in word, he is a perfect man, able also to bridle the whole body. Indeed, we put bits in horses' mouths that they may obey us, and we turn their whole body. Look also at ships: although they are so large and are driven by fierce winds, they are turned by a very small rudder wherever the pilot desires. Even so the tongue is a little member and boasts great things.

See how great a forest a little fire kindles! And the tongue is a fire, a world of iniquity. The tongue is so set among our members that it defiles the whole body, and sets on fire the course of nature; and it is set on fire by hell. For every kind of beast and bird, of reptile and creature of the sea, is tamed and has been tamed by mankind. But no man can tame the tongue. It is an unruly evil, full of deadly poison. With it we bless our God and Father, and with it we curse men, who have been made in the similitude of God. Out of the same mouth proceed blessing and cursing. My brethren, these things ought not to be so. Does a spring send forth fresh water and bitter from the same opening? Can a fig tree, my brethren, bear olives, or a grapevine bear figs? Thus no spring yields both salt water and fresh. (James 3:1-12)

James compares the body of a man to an unrestrained horse. The animal seeks only its passions. In order for the horse to become useful it must be controlled. Left to itself it would never accomplish anything useful. Man, left to himself would never accomplish anything useful.

In order to control and direct a horse we use a bridle. By controlling the tongue of the animal you can control the entire animal. Also, the horse does not bridle itself, he must be directed by an outside force. The same is true for man; he must be controlled by God.

Another analogy is used, a ship's rudder. The emphasis is on the contrast between the size of the rudder and the size of the ship. The small rudder can direct the large ship, even in the fierce wind and storm. Something does not have to be large in order to control us. Even though the tongue is a very small part of our body, it exerts tremendous control over our lives.

The tongue needs an outside source of control, we cannot tame it ourselves. No man can tame his own tongue, but God can. The word *tame* implies force. You cannot tame an animal by using reason. A certain amount of force must be applied. In order to tame you must have the power to restrain. The tongue cannot be tamed because it cannot be restrained.

Sometimes we can control our external actions. However, we have no control over our internal feelings. You get angry at someone but you do not necessarily say or do anything until you get alone with yourself or your spouse and your tongue lets fly your true feelings. The term *poison* also means arrow, and describes the poisonous arrows we shoot with our speech.

A man approached John Wesley and said, "Mr. Wesley, I pride myself in speaking my mind; that is my talent."

Wesley replied, "The Lord wouldn't mind if you buried that talent."

When we commit ourselves to Christ, the poison that is contained in the tongue can be transformed into a blessing, not only for ourselves, but for others also. The way we utilize our tongue, and our speech, provides a test of our faith, and also reveals the power of our faith.

Our Attitude toward the World

> *Adulterers and adulteresses! Do you not know that friendship with the world is enmity with God? Whoever therefore wants to be a friend of the world makes himself an enemy of God.* (James 4:4)

This is a reference to spiritual adultery, not physical. It is based on the Old Testament concept of Israel as the bride of God (see Jeremiah 3:20). To disobey God is like breaking the marriage vows. Our relationship to God is intimate, like a marriage.

If a man is worldly he cannot be godly. No man can serve two masters (see Matthew 6:24). A man may either use the world or be used by the world.

The ermine is a small animal like a mink. The snow-white fur is used to make beautiful fur coats. The animals take particular pleasure in its white fur and will protect it against all hazards. Sometimes, fur hunters will use the animal's instinct to protect the purity of its fur as a snare. They will locate the ermine's den, usually in the cleft of a rock or the hollow of a decaying tree, and coat the entrance with filth. When the dogs chase the ermine it will not enter the soiled home, surrendering its life rather than risking uncleanness.

> We find ourselves being a friend to the world when we have the same interests and goals as the world.

Perhaps this illustrates how far we should be willing to go to stay clean from the world. When James describes *friendship with the world* he does not mean a casual rubbing of shoulders. The Greek word is one of the words for *love* (philia)—the kind of love we have for a friend. Perhaps we could paraphrase it to read, *Do you know that when you fall in love with the world, you begin to hate God?*

Friendship is based on common interests and concerns. We find ourselves being a friend to the world when we have the same interests and goals as the world. We hate to be different so we become like the world. The path of least resistance is conformity. This friendship does not refer to living in the world. We have no choice since God has placed us in the world. Consequently, we will come into contact with the world as the natural course of life.

James is not concerned about an occasional sign of worldliness that happens to us all. Rather, he speaks of an attitude of the heart, the disposition of the soul, the conscious decision to run after the things of the world. The friend of the world *makes himself* an enemy of God. By his own will he takes a stand against God. It is possible to translate it as *declare himself* as an enemy of God. Friendship with the world is an open declaration of our hostility with God.

When we begin to take a genuine interest in things of the world, it is easy and almost inevitable that before long, they have first place in our lives. Some of these things are good, but should never come before God. God is a jealous God, and will not share His love with any other person or thing. The power of our faith determines our attitude toward the world.

Our Attitude toward Prayer (5:13-18)

Is anyone among you suffering? Let him pray. Is anyone cheerful? Let him sing psalms. Is anyone among you sick? Let him call for the elders of the church, and let them pray over him, anointing him with oil in the name of the Lord. And the prayer of faith will save the sick, and the Lord will raise him up. And if he has committed sins, he will be forgiven. Confess your trespasses to one another, and pray for one another, that you may be healed. The effective, fervent prayer of a righteous man avails much. Elijah was a man with a nature like ours, and he prayed earnestly that it would not rain; and it did not rain on the land for three years and six months. And he prayed again, and the heaven gave rain, and the earth produced its fruit. (James 5:13-18)

A final test of the power of our faith concerns our attitude toward prayer. James seems very concerned with our motive when we pray. In communication with God, selfish motives are revealed. This is accomplished in two ways. The first is internally. Within ourselves we know why we are asking. It is the witness of the Holy Spirit helping us understand our desires. We do not have to pray too long for something before God reveals our motives. We may not want to admit our selfishness but we will know.

> The purpose of prayer (as in all activities) is to glorify God.

The second is externally. In case we do not listen to the witness of the Holy Spirit, another evidence of selfish motives is unanswered prayer. It is obvious that if a prayer is not answered, something is wrong. However, if we stay on our knees long enough, then our motives will become pure. Continued fellowship and communication with God will purify our motives.

The purpose of prayer (as in all activities) is to glorify God. We need to examine our prayer list and ask, *Why am I praying for this? Is this for God's glory or for myself?* One of the benefits of prayer is that it helps us to align our desires and motives with God's.

This is one of the ways God tests our faith. Again, let me remind you the test is not for the purpose of giving us a pass or fail grade, but to refine our faith. It is God's way of increasing the power of our faith.

He uses our relationships with others, both believers and non-believers, our attitude toward the things of the world, our faithfulness to good works, our control of the tongue, and our motivations for our prayer life as opportunities for our benefit. In other words, God can use all of life to make our faith strong. Rather than trying to avoid bad experiences and difficult situations, we must open our eyes to see them as opportunities for God to work.

If we are tenacious enough, one day we will find our name listed on the great roll call of faith alongside those mentioned in Hebrews 11. *Count it all joy...* when testing arrives, because the testing of your faith reveals the power of your faith.

Chapter 10

Keeping Your Faith Powerful

For it was so, when Solomon was old, that his wives turned his heart after other gods; and his heart was not loyal to the Lord his God, as was the heart of his father David. (1 Kings 11:4)

On September 11th, we all watched in horror as two of the largest structures ever built by man, crumbled to the ground in less than two hours. Every time we watch the replay of this massive destruction we are reminded of the fact that everything about life is very temporary. More than 5,000 people, who were in the midst of what they probably considered a typical day, are now gone. Tens of thousands of family members and friends also had their worlds shattered. Our nation, and the world, was forever changed as the twin towers of the World Trade Center came crashing to the earth.

However, no structure built by modern man can ever surpass the temple constructed under Solomon's leadership. Solomon's temple was certainly one of the most magnificent structures man has ever constructed. It was certainly not large by today's standards, only 60 ft. wide and 135 ft. long and 45 ft. high.

Around the outside walls were three stories of rooms and chambers for storage. The inside was paneled with cedar, floored with cypress and inlaid with gold. It was decorated with the finest, most expensive jewels of the day. It took thousands of craftsmen and laborers seven years to complete the project.

It was perhaps the most expensive building ever built and would far exceed any contemporary structure in elegance. Solomon was the wealthiest man in the world and the temple was sufficient evidence of his great wealth.

One of the great tragedies in history was the destruction of this temple by the Babylonians in 587 BC. Although it had suffered neglect and deterioration, to stand by and see this mighty structure brought down must have been a terrible sight.

However, an even greater tragedy than the destruction of Solomon's temple was the deterioration of the man Solomon. When the temple was destroyed the Bible does not even require an entire verse to describe the event - Then they burned the house of God... (2 Chronicles 36:19). An entire chapter (I Kings 11) is devoted to describing the destruction of the man who built the temple.

When we think of Solomon we usually focus upon the good qualities he possessed. Solomon is known for many things:

- **Influence**

So Solomon reigned over all kingdoms from the River to the land of the Philistines, as far as the border of Egypt. They brought tribute and served Solomon all the days of his life. (1 Kings 4:21)

- **Wisdom**

And God gave Solomon wisdom and exceedingly great understanding, and largeness of heart like the sand on the seashore. (1 Kings 4:29)

- **Wealth**

So King Solomon surpassed all the kings of the earth in riches and wisdom. (1 Kings 10:23)

It is important however, that we do not forget the final chapter of his life. That chapter is recorded for us in the Word of God to teach us an important lesson about the destruction of the man. As we watch the replay of his destruction, we learn a valuable lesson about our own lives.

The last thing that is said about Solomon, the wisest man who ever lived, is that *his heart was turned away from the Lord...* (I Kings 11:9). What a tragic epitaph for such a great man. The greatest threat to the power of our faith is losing our single-minded devotion to God. Solomon allowed his devotion to God to be diluted by the world.

Source of Deterioration

Several factors contributed to the deterioration of Solomon's devotion to God; chief among them was lusting after the way of the world. In spite of being the wisest man in the world, Solomon's downfall was precipitated by his desire for the things of the world. In the end, he sought to be a king just like the world's kings. The king of God's people was to be unique, to live by different standards.

> *But he shall not multiply horses for himself, nor cause the people to return to Egypt to multiply horses, for the Lord has said to you, 'You shall not return that way again.' Neither shall he multiply wives for himself, lest his heart turn away; nor shall he greatly multiply silver and gold for himself.* (Deuteronomy 17:16-17)

He was to be different in terms of trust. He was forbidden to accumulate horses and develop a massive army for protection. Yet, we are told that *Solomon had 40,000 stalls of horses for his chariots, and 12,000 horsemen* (1 Kings 4:26).

Also, he was not to have multiple wives, which were primarily for the purpose of political alliances. But, Solomon had seven hundred wives, princesses, and three hundred concubines, and his wives turned his heart away (1 Kings 11:3). It would have been difficult to have so many wives but Solomon's problem was compounded by the fact that he *loved many foreign women* (1 Kings 11:1). His wives were not from among God's people. These women are credited with *turning his heart away after other gods...* Their ways were not God's ways. Their devotion was not to God.

Solomon not only invited them into his household; he listened to their words and followed their ways. The practice of taking foreign wives was expressly forbidden by God in a direct command.

> *Nor shall you make marriages with them. You shall not give your daughter to their son, nor take their daughter for your son. For they will turn your sons away from following Me, to serve other gods; so the anger of the Lord will be aroused against you and destroy you suddenly.* (Deuteronomy 7:3-4)

His first wife was an Egyptian who had converted to being a follower of God. This initial act of disobedience, which from man's perspective turned out fine, opened the door for further defiance. Perhaps in the first two or three instances he hoped to convert these women. However, after tearing down the fence of God's law, Solomon roamed freely in forbidden territory, taking hundreds of wives in disobedience. Not only did he take these wives but also *Solomon held fast to these in love* (1 Kings 11:2).

> *from the nations of whom the Lord had said to the children of Israel, "You shall not intermarry with them, nor they with you. Surely they will turn away your hearts after their gods." Solomon clung to these in love. (1 Kings 11:2)*

Israel's king was not to increase silver and gold *for himself*. God would make the nation rich but the king was not to seek wealth. But again, listen to the description of Solomon's wealth: All King Solomon's drinking vessels were of gold, and all the vessels of the house of the forest of Lebanon were of pure gold. None was of silver; it was not considered valuable in the days of Solomon (1 Kings 10:21). Solomon sought and acquired all of these things in his desire for the ways of the world. Solomon defiantly left the ways of God.

There is a process of deterioration of metal that is known as corrosion or rust. We all know what rust looks like as it can literally eat up a piece of metal until it disappears. Rust occurs when metal is placed in a hostile environment. Metal is especially vulnerable to air and salt water, and in areas with high humidity rust is a major problem.

Deterioration of the Christian life also begins by being in the wrong environment, by placing ourselves in an environment that is hostile to our faith.

Deterioration of the Christian life also begins by being in the wrong environment, by placing ourselves in an environment that is hostile to our faith. If you find yourself lusting after the ways of the world, or listening to the words of the world, or leaving the ways of the Lord then your devotion to God will soon be deteriorating.

To a certain extent all Christians must nurture faith in a hostile environment. We are forced to live out our faith in the world. However, there is also an element of control that we can have over that environment. We make many decisions each day, which alter that environment. We choose the places we go, the people we associate with, and the words we listen to. All of these elements can be sources of deterioration in our spiritual lives. The power of our faith in God is key to the prevention of spiritual deterioration.

Significance of Deterioration

The deterioration of Solomon's commitment was significant because it meant that *his heart was not wholly devoted to the Lord his God...* It caused Solomon to have a diluted devotion. In order to be a great man or woman of faith, out attention must be focused solely upon God and His Word. Solomon allowed his attention to be divided between God and the gods of his wives. Consequently he *did not follow the Lord fully...* (11:6).

Instead of giving all of his time and effort to serving and pleasing God, Solomon was busy building temples and worship places for the pagan gods.

> *For Solomon went after Ashtoreth the goddess of the Sidonians, and after Milcom the abomination of the Ammonites. Solomon did evil in the sight of the Lord, and did not fully follow the Lord, as did his father David. Then Solomon built a high place for Chemosh the abomination of Moab, on the hill that is east of Jerusalem, and for Molech the abomination of the people of Ammon. And he did likewise for all his foreign wives, who burned incense and sacrificed to their gods. (1 Kings 11:5-8).*

These other gods provided a powerful force for diluting his devotion to God.

Once Solomon diluted his devotion to God then he suffered through a very dangerous demise of his kingdom and his life.

So the Lord became angry with Solomon, because his heart had turned from the Lord God of Israel, who had appeared to him twice, and had commanded him concerning this thing, that he should not go after other gods; but he did not keep what the Lord had commanded. Therefore the Lord said to Solomon, "Because you have done this, and have not kept My covenant and My statutes, which I have commanded you, I will surely tear the kingdom away from you and give it to your servant. (1 Kings 11:9-11).

Solomon had now come full circle from his younger days. Solomon was to blame for the loss of the kingdom of Israel. It took several generations, but the course established by Solomon ultimately led to the demise of the entire nation.

It is foolish to allow our devotion to God to be watered down. I believe it is safe to say that the majority of Christians possess a diluted devotion to God. At some point in their lives they committed themselves totally to God. At the moment of salvation they truly gave all of themselves to Jesus, making him Lord of their lives. However, like Solomon, with the passing of time, that complete devotion to God has become diluted by the world. If our devotion has been diluted then we should not expect to escape the same consequences that affected Solomon. When our devotion to God becomes diluted, the power of our faith in God is weakened.

Solution to Deterioration

Buried within the final phrase of this verse is the solution to a deteriorating devotion to God. The heart of Solomon *was not as the heart of David his father had been.* Solomon did what was evil in the sight of the LORD, and did not follow the LORD fully, as David his father had done (1 Kings 11:6). David is an example of one who kept his devotion to God pure and undiluted.

We could spend a long time studying the life of David to learn why he was considered *a man after God's own heart.* However, let's simply note some contrasts between David and Solomon that allowed him to maintain a pure devotion to God.

The sins of David are carefully detailed in Scripture, but they differ from those of Solomon. David is characterized by momentary sins of passion, i.e. his encounter with Bathsheba. After the sin, he exemplifies great remorse and sorrow. The sins of Solomon seem to be more the sins of the heart and ongoing problems with idolatry.

It took Solomon 7 years to build the temple for God (1 Kings 6:38), but it required 13 years to build a palace for himself (1 Kings 7:1). David accumulated great amounts of money but it was for the purpose of building the temple. Solomon accumulated even greater sums of money but it was for his own benefit.

As sinful as he was, David is never criticized for building pagan temples or worshipping idols. His faith always remained true to the One True God. David was a man, a sinful man, yet he was faithful to God. From the very beginning of his rule, Solomon was noted for his worship of false gods.

And Solomon loved the Lord, walking in the statutes of his father David, except that he sacrificed and burned incense at the high places. (1 Kings 3:3)

I would like to offer a simple three point process to help you to keep your devotion to God pure and undiluted.

First, deal immediately with sin. Sin is like leaven, ever expanding and permeating into our lives. When we allow any sin to remain in our lives it will ultimately bring about our destruction. Sin is like adding water to the medicine; it dilutes our devotion until it is worthless.

Second, maintain the proper attitude about things. We must never believe that God allows us to have things just for our own benefit. He entrusts things to us for our stewardship. When our attitude about things is wrong then our devotion will be to those possessions instead of to God.

Third, keep your heart free from other gods. Carefully guard your heart against devotion to anything other than God. Only one thing can have first place in your life. You must carefully guard your heart from devotion to any other person, possession or power.

Keep your heart with all diligence, For out of it spring the issues of life. (Proverbs 4:23)

It is ironic that Solomon is credited with writing these words. If you will diligently follow these three simple steps then you can maintain a single-minded devotion to God, and you will experience the power of faith.

Conclusion

A Beyond Faith

The great British preacher Martyn-Lloyd Jones said, *Faith is the refusal to panic.* We have studied the great biblical heroes of the faith, and it is easy to see that panic might have been an appealing option for each of them. I know it is frequently the option we choose.

Facing the difficult times of life can be overwhelming and cause us to throw up our arms in surrender. In fact, that is one of the things that has been disappointing as a pastor; seeing the number of people who give up and walk away in the midst of struggling.

> *Now it happened, on a certain day, that He got into a boat with His disciples. And He said to them, "Let us cross over to the other side of the lake." And they launched out. But as they sailed He fell asleep. And a windstorm came down on the lake,*

and they were filling with water, and were in jeopardy. And they came to Him and awoke Him, saying, "Master, Master, we are perishing!"

Then He arose and rebuked the wind and the raging of the water. And they ceased, and there was a calm. But He said to them, "Where is your faith?"

And they were afraid, and marveled, saying to one another, "Who can this be? For He commands even the winds and water, and they obey Him!" (Luke 8:22-25)

Jesus, along with His Disciples, climbed in a boat to cross the lake. Jesus went to sleep and left the navigation to the Disciples. Even when a storm arose, a serious enough storm to cause these experienced fishermen to panic, Jesus remained asleep.

When they woke Him with the warning they were about to die, Jesus simply stood up, and rebuked the wind and water, and everything returned to calm. The way the story reads, we get the impression that the Disciples were even more frightened by the power of Jesus than they were of the storm. Jesus' response to the storm was much different than the Disciples. He shows that faith may calm the storm, or it might calm us in the midst of the storm.

The key to this story is Jesus' question, *Where is your faith*? In other words, the reason they were frightened is because their faith was weak. The previous quote that *faith is the refusal to panic*, is essentially a reminder of what Jesus was teaching the Disciples. In the midst of storms, our faith allows us not to panic. We may not know what God is going to do or how He is going to do it, but faith says God is in control.

I didn't have any idea when I started writing this book titled, *The Power of Your Faith* that God would use it to help me through the unexpected crisis of my brother's death. I came away from this crisis thanking God for preparing me for what He knew, and I didn't know would take place before the concluding chapter of this book would be written. I can say without hesitation that it was the power of my faith in God that helped me cope with his sudden death, and to move forward in a difficult time.

During this time, I kept rehearsing in my mind what I've called, *a beyond faith*, a faith that enables me to see beyond the circumstances of my life; a faith that enables me to see beyond the consequences of my life; and a faith that enables me to see beyond the conclusion of my life. A beyond faith looks beyond the now to a future with God in heaven. This *beyond faith* exceeded beyond what I saw, what I felt, what I thought, what I knew, and what I could do. I am convicted even more in the fact that the power of my faith in God matters in life and in death.

A *beyond faith* will move us beyond the circumstances of this world that so quickly and easily drag us down.

I believe in my heart that God wanted me to write this book from the series of sermons I preached, titled, *The Power of Your Faith in God*. I also believe God wants to use this book to encourage, strengthen, and to give hope to others who will place their faith in Him.

About the Author

Dr. Howard E. Anderson, Sr. was born in Jewett, Texas. After graduating from George Washington Carver High School, he served in the United States Air Force and is a Vietnam War veteran. Howard organized The "Exciting" Singing Hills Baptist Church in January 1984, with 24 members, and has served as Pastor for 31 years. Under his leadership the congregation has grown to over 3,000 members and completed five building projects.

In 1983, Dr. Anderson became the first African American to receive a degree from Criswell College. That year, he received his B.A. in Biblical Studies. He received an M.A. in Pastoral Theology in 1993, also from Criswell College. In 2003, he received his Doctorate of Ministry from Bethany Divinity College and Seminary in Dothan, Alabama.

Dr. Anderson has been active in Denominational activities, serving in leadership positions at several levels. He has also served as a Trustee of Dallas Southwest Medical Center.

In 2003, Dr. Anderson wrote his first book *Growth Principles for an Exciting Church*, discussing the mental discernment every church needs to be alive and vibrant. In 2005 he released his second book *Life Navigation: Biblical Guidance For Daily Living*, expounding the normal, cooperative, and continual aspects of spiritual growth, and how God's Word guides through our journey.

Dr. Anderson has been married to Mrs. Shirley Von Anderson for 49 years. They have one son, Howard Jr., M.D., daughter-in-law Erica, granddaughter Francesca Von, and grandsons Howard III and William Albert.

CPSIA information can be obtained
at www.ICGtesting.com
Printed in the USA
FFHW011844220919
55137238-60862FF

9 780990 347750